Entrepreneurship
A Hands-on Guide to Starting your Business

About the Author

Muthu is a parallel entrepreneur having been involved in several start-ups over last 20 years. He has over 25 years of experience in Engineering, Management and Entrepreneurship. He has a MBA in Multimedia Finance and his passion is in Entrepreneurial Development, Mentoring, Management of Emerging Technologies and Innovation.

Muthu's first-degree is in Engineering. He is a British Trained Chartered Electrical Engineer and Chartered Member (IET UK), a Chartered Engineer (Engineering Council, UK) and a European Engineer (European Federation of National Engineering Associations). Muthu is also a former professor in Management. Muthu has been a judge and mentor in many business plan competitions including IIM, IIT, Power of IDEAS, HSBC Business Plan Competition, McKinsey's and several others in the last 20 years.

Muthu is the founder of the VibaZone and Blue Equator Leadership, Innovation and Entrepreneurship Foundation (BELIEF). He is working on a Virtual International Business Accelerator aka VibaZone based in several locations. The vision is to develop and provide a virtual community of entrepreneurs or anyone wishing to participate in building or growing a sustainable business in any area or industry. Muthu is also currently the CEO, Incubation, Healthcare Technology Innovation Centre (HTIC), at Indian Institute of Technology Madras (IITM).

He was responsible for developing the Malaysian National Unipreneur Development Programme (NUDP) at the Multimedia Development Corporation (MDC). He has mentored, consulted and facilitated participants from various parts of the world including companies like British Telecom, Institute of Public Administration, Malaysia and many more. Currently, he is the innovation driver for several companies and universities in India and Malaysia.

Entrepreneurship
A Hands-on Guide to Starting your Business

Muthu Singaram
Founder
VibaZone and Blue Equator Leadership
Innovation and Entrepreneurship Foundation (BELIEF)
CEO, Incubation, Healthcare Technology Innovation Centre (HTIC),
at Indian Institute of Technology Madras (IITM)

DeDicAteD to

This book is in the memory of my dear friends who are no more and have left prematurely

1. Francis Xavier, my dear friend and senior at primary school in Ipoh, Malaysia.

2. Michael Scott, my dear friend and dorm mate back in boarding school in North of Ireland.

3. Marie Cheng, my dear friend and hang-out mate in Ipoh, Malaysia.

4. K S Kok, my dear friend and colleague at Carsem Semiconductor in Ipoh, Malaysia.

5. Gurucharan Singh, my dear friend and Physician in Ipoh, Malaysia.

contents

Preface — *xiii*
Acknowledgement — *xv*

PArt i   entrePreneuriAL triGGer Points

Chapter 1   Entrepreneurial Ticker — 3

    Passion and Motivation — 4
    Vision, Mission, Goals, Objectives — 4
    Who and What is an Entrepreneur? — 5
    Key Elements of Entrepreneurial Success — 5
    Education and Entrepreneurship — 6
    Why Promote Entrepreneurship? — 6
    What Does It Take to be an Entrepreneur? — 6
    Demands of an Entrepreneur — 7
    Key Factors That Can Influence Entrepreneurship — 7
    Positives and Negatives of Being an Entrepreneur — 8
    Forms of Entrepreneurship — 8
    Life Cycle of a Venture — 9

Chapter 2   Entrepreneurial Response to Challenge — 11

Chapter 3   Entrepreneurs' Tools to Determine Ideas — 19

    Determining by Systematic Approach — 23
    Determining by Market Approach — 24

Chapter 4   Entrepreneurial Vehicle for Success — 27

    Formation of a Team — 27

Business as a Legal Entity 29
Which Structure is Right for You? 30

PArt ii   entrePreneuriAL FLourish: GettinG A FinAnciAL GriP

Chapter 5   Source of Funding and Support 37
Why Do You Need Funding? 37
Sources of Funding 37
Which Source is Best for You? 41
How to Get Help? 42

Chapter 6   Basic Accounting 43
Some Fundamental Concepts 43
Accounting – The Systematic Way 44
The Double Entry System (Dual Aspect Concept) 45

Chapter 7   Different Types of Taxes in India 59
A Brief Overview of the Tax Structure in India 59

Chapter 8   Costing 61
Cost Control and Reduction 61

Chapter 9   Return on Investment 67
Financial Ratio Analysis 67

Chapter 10   Understanding Financial Plan 73
Why a Financial Plan? 73
Financial Report 73
Break-Even Point Analysis 74
Ratio Analysis 74
Managing Cash Flow 76
Understanding Cash Flow 76
Cash Flow Budget 77

PArt iii   entrePreneurAL DriVe: MArKetinG

Chapter 11   Entrepreneurial Marketing — 81
- What is Marketing? — 81
- Marketing Strategies — 82
- 4C's of Marketing — 83
- 4A's of Marketing — 83
- Product Mix — 83
- Product Strategy Mix — 84
- The ANSOFF Matrix — 84

Chapter 12   Entrepreneurial Marketing Research — 87
- Methods of Market Research — 87
- Ways to Do Human Touch Research — 87

Chapter 13   Entrepreneurial Marketing Plan — 89
- Complete Marketing Plan — 89
- Multi-Level Marketing (MLM) and Franchising — 94

PArt iV   entrePreneuriAL PLAnninG

Chapter 14   Entrepreneurial Business Plan — 97
- The Importance of a Business Plan — 97
- Components of a Business Plan — 97

Chapter 15   Entrepreneurial Power Presentation — 101
- The Objectives of a Power Presentation — 101
- What Can a Power Presentation Do for You? — 101
- The Components of a Power Presentation — 101
- Basic Guidelines — 102
- Visceral Pitch — 105

Chapter 16   Entrepreneurial Strategic Planning — 107
- First W of Strategy — 107
- Second W of Strategy — 108

	Third W of Strategy	108
	Fourth W of Strategy	109
	The 10 Step Planning Process	109

Chapter 17   Entrepreneurial Project Management   111

	What is a Project?	111
	What is Project Management?	111
	Why Project Management?	111
	History of Project Management	111
	What is Good Project Management?	112
	How to Manage a Project?	112
	How Not to Manage a Project?	112
	Project Planning	112
	Elements of Planning	113
	Project Management Software	115

PArt V   entrePreneuriAL reAL AnD VirtuAL WorLD oF inForMAtion

Chapter 18   How Entrepreneurs can Use Technology to Benefit   119

	Benefits of Technology	119
	The Internet	120

Chapter 19   Valuable Reading   121

	Time and Efficiency	121
	Setting Goals	121
	Problem Solving	121
	Leadership	122
	Communication	122
	Delegation	122
	General Interest	122
	Team Building	122

Chapter 20   Websites to Visit   125

PArt Vi entrePreneuriAL JuGALbAnDi

Chapter 21	**Entrepreneurial Means of Protecting the Fruits of Labour**	**131**
	Intellectual Property	131
	Why Intellectual Property?	132
	Generally	137
	Important Bodies	137
Chapter 22	**Entrepreneurial Ethics**	**139**
	Anand Corporate Services Limited	140
	Aptech Limited	140
	Avon Cycle Limited	141
	CISCO System Inc.	141
	ICICI Bank Ltd	141
	Infosys Technologies Limited	141
	ITC Limited	142
	Mahindra & Mahindra	142
	Dalmia Cement (Bharat) Limited	143
	DCM Shriram Consolidated Limited	143
Chapter 23	**Entrepreneurial Talent Management**	**145**
	Talent Management: A Living Definition	145
	Why Talent Management Today?	146
	The Major Drivers for Talent Management	146
Chapter 24	**Entrepreneurial Mentoring**	**149**
	Mentoring, Coaching, Training	149
	Types of Mentoring	149
	The Mentoring Process	150
	Principles of Good Mentoring	150
Chapter 25	**Entrepreneurial Alternatives**	**153**
	Steps in Buying a Business	153

	Deal Structuring	154
	Business Management Succession	154
Chapter 26	**Entrepreneurial Learning from Other Entrepreneurs**	**155**
	Dhirubhai Ambani	155
	Rahul Kumar Bajaj	156
	Ratan Tata	156
	Kiran Mazumdar Shaw	157
	Narayana Murthy	157
	Azim Premji	158
	KB Chandrasekhar	158
	Vinod Khosla	159
Chapter 27	**Entrepreneurial Mindset**	**161**
Chapter 28	**Sharing My Entrepreneurial Experience for the Benefit of Other Entrepreneurs**	**163**
	The MBS Principle	163

PreFAce

Why write another book on Entrepreneurship when there are so many available in the book shelves of the book stores around the world?

This book is well overdue. I have been toying with the idea of writing this book for more than ten years and decided it was high time I put my experience on paper. I am glad I delayed this book for ten years as with what I know today I am embarrassed by what I knew ten years ago and I am sure I will be even more embarrassed in another ten years as I learn even more. Entrepreneurship is a learning process which will evolve over the years.

Most books in shelves are written by non-practicing entrepreneurs as practicing entrepreneurs have no time. I, on the other hand, have been going around talking about entrepreneurship as an entrepreneur.

I have included several chapters in this book, which are unique in nature. These include a chapter on my personal experience, mentoring, websites and books which can help an entrepreneur. I hope to customise some chapters according to the countries where this book is published so you will get a local book and not a foreign book.

This is written for the knowledge of entrepreneurship to be shared around the world and for this very reason a download of my lectures and powerpoint presentations on this subject comes with this book for teachers to use while teaching this subject.

The income from this book will go to my newly formed trust "**Bluê Equator Lêadêrship Innovation and Entrêprênêurship Foundation**" (BELIEF) and will be used to support activities which promote learning for the more underprivileged in India, the country of my origin as well as my adopted country.

We have made changes to Chapter 7 to take into account GST.

This book discusses with you at a personal level, to spur your thought and generate learning unlike other books in this area which are too academic.

This is a very short book so you should be able to read it in a few days and start applying on your project.

This book is based on the many lectures and seminars wherein I have been a speaker and what I have learnt from these.

You, the reader, might say all authors say their book is unique, I leave that call in your hand, my valued reader.

If you find this book useful, let us build on it but if you find it is rubbish, please forget about it. Thank you for reading this humble book.

MUTHU SINGARAM

AcKnoWLeDGeMent

This book was only possible because of the education, experience, love, guidance and support of my parents (Singaram and Unnamalai) provided to me unlike many others. I pray to the almighty GOD that every child is blessed like me.

I could not have possibly done justice to this book if not for the love and support of my darling wife Chittu and our two sons, who were kids during the initial release of the book, are now almost young adults making their own mark. I thank the almighty GOD for having given me this wonderful family.

Others who have constantly supported me are both my in-laws (Nagarajan and Meena), in particular my father-in-law who has been a great support and a guide to me in India and my ever-willing sister Kalyani for her support. A big thanks to my Uncle-in-law (TK Chetty) who suffered to correct this manuscript.

My many colleagues and friends, in particular my dear friend professor S Srikanath, who helped in crafting portions of this book.

This book would not have been possible if it weren't for many of my students, not only at SMOT class of 2009, but at all places who have done research for some chapters and to many of the world's best schools and participants in my many seminars around the world. This was only possible because many heads of schools and seminar organisers gave me that opportunity to deliver my lectures.

I must record my sincere gratitude to four of my dear friends who have promoted my book and work in Canada Colin Dodds (President Emeritus, Professor of Finance, Saint Mary's University, Halifax, Canada), Kevin Schwenker, Dave Watters and Dawnita Spac which has led to numerous engagements in North America.

Jasmine Kway my dear friend who has promoted my book and work in Singapore which has led to numerous engagements in Singapore.

I must make a special mention to two other dear friends of mine Ashok Jhunjhunwala (Professor, IIT Madras, India, Advisor, Minister of Power and MNRE, Government of India) and Ghauth Jasmon (Former VC, University of Malaya, Malaysia) both of whom have been great mentors to me.

I thank the VibaZone team both present and past in Canada, India and Malaysia, Mohamed Siddique Hamzah in Malaysia, Hameed Rahamathullah and Prathistha Jain for their enormous energy and bearing with me as often as it can be a challenge working with me.

.

MUTHU SINGARAM

Part I

Entrepreneurial Trigger Points

Chapter 1: Entrepreneurial Ticker

> *"The special gallium arsenide gun, schottky barrier mixer diodes, compact comparator for antenna system – India was banned from buying any one of these high technology devices, but innovation cannot be suppressed by international restrictions".*
>
> - A passage from *Wings of Fire: An Autobiography*
> - **APJ Abdul Kalam** with **Arun Tiwari**

At the start of this book let us try and explore the solution to this question "Are entrepreneurs born or made?" My response to this age old question is, it is a bit of both. Traits like attitude are inbuilt but skills like conflict resolution, presentation–these come with experience.

The best way to describe an entrepreneur would be to say he is the one who sees an opportunity and builds an enterprise out of it.

Entrepreneurship is becoming an increasingly popular career choice in the current economic slow down. If you are planning to become an entrepreneur you will not be alone and will have plenty of company.

Many have gone the entrepreneural route due to external factors including layoffs, frustration with their current workplace culture, or a need for greater flexibility in their lives. However, it is most important to go with your own internal factors which include passion, wanting to be independent, wanting to accomplish, building an enterprise, enjoy freedom, a burning desire to make a profession out of a hobby or enjoy the challenges.

Entrepreneurship is not for all. You may most likely be aware that many new ventures fail and probably one out of three will not be in business after five years. The dotcoms were successes of the late 90s and early 2000s, but it is most unlikely that you will become successful overnight. It requires hard work, determination, vision, need to dedicate long hours and endless energy which is more realistic in today's entrepreneurship.

There is no fixed pattern for entrepreneurship; so long as you are focused and hard-working, your dream can become a reality and you can reap the benefits of entrepreneurship.

> The first thing as an entrepreneur you must be able to ask yourself is, what you want because if you do not ask, you do not get.

To demonstrate this, wherever I speak I always like to start with the following exercise to set off the audience thinking that entrepreneurship has no bars expect the ones you put up.

> **Muthu to Audience:** Someone please give me a red lipstick.
>
> Audience goes silent.
>
> **Muthu:** Do not worry! I shall return it without using it.
>
> Audience laughs and someone gives the red lipstick to Muthu.
>
> **Muthu:** Someone from the audience, please give me a hundred rupees.
>
> Again Audience goes silent but someone in the audience does give the hundred rupees.
>
> **Muthu:** Give me a bunch of car keys.
>
> Someone in audience gives them to Muthu.
>
> **Muthu:** How did I get all these things?
>
> Audience thinks deeply and in complex terms for a response.
>
> **Muthu:** Please do not think too deep!
>
> Audience laughs and finally someone says "You asked for them!"
>
> **Muthu:** Excellent!

Why do i do this?

To show the audience you will get only if you ask for something. What is the worst case? You will not get, and that is no different from where you started. So why worry - always as entrepreneurs ask for what you want and you will get it.

PAssion AnD MotiVAtion

These are two major players in an entrepreneur's life. Unless you have passion you will not drive your venture forward. To have passion, "one must be motivated" so you see they are somewhat related to each other. How to be passionate? This happens when you have a genuine interest to listen to your customer and market, being innovative, having a product to sell, paying attention to details, being a driving force, using the ideas yourself, engaging with the market, fixing issues and redefining your ideas. All these happen when you are motivated. How to be motivated? Be inspired, set goals, network, reward yourself for successes and exercise to rejuvenate yourself. Hence passion is maintained by being motivated.

Vision, Mission, GoALs, obJectiVes

Before embarking on anything, you should be clear in your mind with your vision, mission, goals and objective statements.

Vision is the big picture of what you are trying to do and it must have a time line. Mission is how you are going to go about achieving this vision. Goals are long- term and objectives are short- term and these must have numbers in order to get you closer to your vision. Believe me, all four are different and they are NOT the same. However they are inter-linked to one another. These must be specific, measurable, attainable, real, timely, personal, and positive and above all they must be written down so you do not divert from what you set out to achieve and it will also serve as a road map to you.

> **Do you want to be an entrepreneur?**
>
> Obviously you want to or you would not have acquired this book.
>
> But I say –SAY NO.
>
> Why do I say this?
>
> In my seminars I get answers like "do not know" etc. but the best is "You do not want others to be entrepreneurs because you want to keep it to yourself." It is weird why I would be going around talking about it if I did not want anyone to be an entrepreneur.

My reason for you to say NO - this is the hardest thing you will ever have to do to be an entrepreneur– to say good old NO. Is it hard to say "NO"? Try it! absolutely, NOT at all.

Who AnD WhAt is An entrePreneur?

I am not going to attempt to tell you what this is or who an entrepreneur is except this beautiful quote which I came across many many years ago:

> *"Anyone who wants to experience the deep, dark canyons of uncertainty and ambiguity; and who wants to walk the breathtaking highlights of success. But I caution, do not plan to walk the latter, until you have experienced the former."*
>
> **An entrepreneur**

Key eLeMents oF entrePreneuriAL success

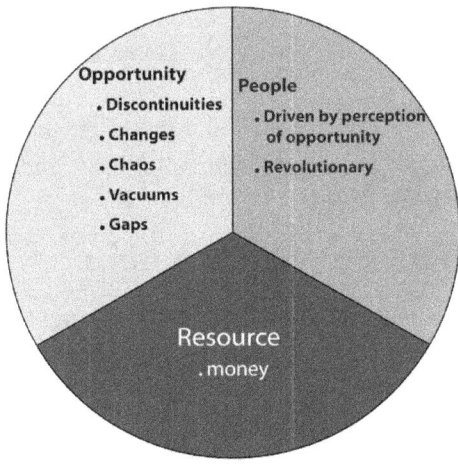

There are three major elements which can lead to an entrepreneurial success. These are

1. Opportunities – which I will cover in detail in the coming chapters;
2. People – without whom nothing can work and
3. Resources.

Once the former two are in place the latter falls into place without too much difficulty.

The late Professor Jeffry A. Timmons, the Franklin W. Olin Distinguished Professor in Entrepreneurship at Babson College said entrepreneurs are high, both in creativity and in management, unlike others.

We often know what we are lacking and will form a team and get on with it. No one said entrepreneurship is a one man show, it is a team effort.

eDucAtion AnD entrePreneurshiP

It is worth noting that success comes to those with knowledge of the subject. How does one get knowledge? Simply by educating oneself and this can be in many forms. How does one educate oneself? Education is drawn from others, our own experience, by going to a class, reading, discussion and many other ways. Hence let me say again, the knowledge you have in the area you are going to be an entrepreneur would be the key to your success.

Why ProMote entrePreneurshiP?

Entrepreneurs create jobs, new industries, equity and great leaders and also contribute to the society. These in turn makes a country economically powerful like America and leads to social mobility.

In today's world which is becoming flatter due to opening of countries and technology, increasing competitiveness and mature products, there is an urgent need for creativity and entrepreneurship. Fortunately the route to becoming an entrepreneur is becoming much more attractive and easier especially since there is a shift from a predominantly manufacturing to a service based economy. Due to this, cost and barriers to entry for entrepreneurs have lowered considerably. It is worthy to note that new ventures are job creators like the Silicon Valley, in San Francisco Silicon Alley, in New York, Route 128 in Boston and industrial parks are the envy of the world.

Entrepreneurship serves as an anchor to many businesses and economy. It can also play a major role in alleviating problems of poverty, unemployment and underemployment in many developing countries in today's world.

WhAt Does it tAKe to be An entrePreneur?

Most of us want to be entrepreneurs but only a few make it. Entrepreneurship is not about starting a couple of business and leaving them. It is about **attitude and the drive** one has. Success does not come just because you went to the top school or is an expert; it comes by that inner drive and passion.

The late Professor Jeffry A. Timmons and his colleagues identified some important entrepreneurial characteristics of successful enterprise owners which still feature in many entrepreneurship studies. I have tried to apply some of these to my personal experience which I am sharing with you now.

As entrepreneurs we have very high levels of drive and abundance of energy. We are always on the go looking how to make good. We have tremendous self-belief. If you do not believe in yourself who else will? We are looking for long- term involvement and use money only as a measure. We do not stop because of problems. We love problem solving and if there is no problem there is no opportunity. We take calculated risks. Who does not take risks? We all do but we think through like crossing the road. We set goals and because of this we are able to deal with failure and love feedbacks to improve. We have high initiative and are responsible. We do not need to be told what to do. We are always doing things. We are able to manage and use resources well plus we compete against our self. We have good internal control and can tolerate ambiguity unlike most people.

I will share with you the MBS aka MUST, BE and SHOULD of an entrepreneur in a later chapter.

DeMAnDs oF An entrePreneur

Again, based on a study by the late Professor Jeffry A. Timmons and his colleagues, they identified some important demands. I am again applying this to my personal experience -

We need to give all to the venture and have complete commitment along with creativity and innovation. As pointed out earlier, knowledge of the subject is crucial. We must be able to build teams who can deliver. Success leads to economic values but it must be accompanied by ethics, integrity and reliability.

Key FActors thAt cAn inFLuence entrePreneurshiP

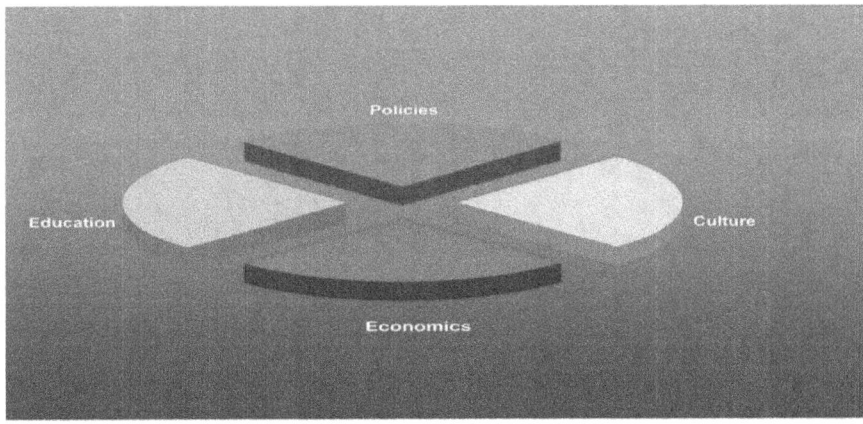

There are four factors which play a major role. These are Policies, Education, Economics and Culture aka PEEC.

a) Favourable policies from policy makers like the Government, schools and others can help entrepreneurial development.

b) As I have already said earlier, education will help influence entrepreneurial development.

c) In the USA, many entrepreneurs make many times the amount of money they invest on their project, 'if the environment allows this. More and more people will get into the entrepreneurs' world as it has economic value.

d) Last but not the least some cultures encourage entrepreneurs. For others it is taboo and they make fun of those who fail. Many of our parents want us to join the Government or a MNC so that our jobs are secure.

PEEC can create the environment for entrepreneurs to be bred.

PositiVes AnD neGAtives oF beinG An entrePreneur

On the positive side, firstly, we are doing something that we enjoy doing, by putting our talent to use. Secondly, we are in control of our future and hence get the satisfaction of making our own money.

On the negative side, life is hard because of irregular income and of having to do all the work ourselves.

ForMs oF entrePreneurshiP

These days many people speak about entrepreneurship—it can be in the form of a profitable enterprise, a non-profitable enterprise, a rural enterprise or a government enterprise. A profitable enterprise is one started for making profits for the founders, a non-profitable enterprise is started to serve the public, a rural enterprise is started to benefit people in rural areas and a government enterprise is started by the government for the benefit of its people. We then have first generation and second generation entrepreneurs. As the words suggest the former is starting out fresh and the latter is when the family is already in the field. There is no reason why one is more successful than the other and similarly no reason why one is more prone to failure than the other.

LiFe cycLe oF A Venture

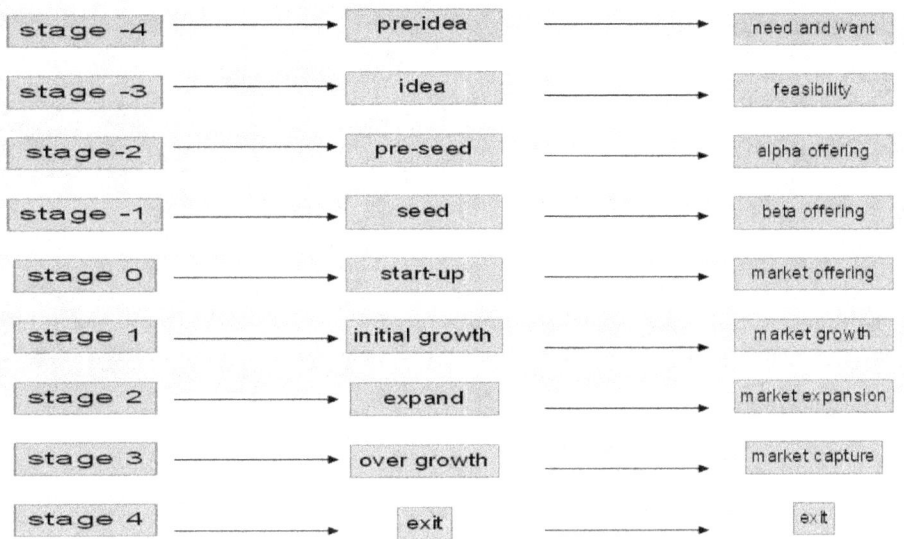

Now let us explore how we get started. I believe that there are nine stages in starting a venture. I have identified them from stage –4 to stage 4. We will take a look at each of these stages one by one.

stage–4 or Pre-idea

This is the first thing we need to do. For our venture to be successful there must be a need or a want. Unless one of this exists, our venture will have no value. A need is a necessity and a want is a desire. Example, water is a necessity and orange juice is a want.

stage–3 or idea

Next we need to study the feasibility of this want and need to formulate our idea. It is absolutely useless unless the idea is feasible and has the potential to be successful.

stage–2 or Pre-seed

Next we start the alpha offering. We start putting the venture together to test if there are takers, usually asking people we know.

stage–1 or seed

Next we start the beta offering. We start pilot runs and offer to a few outside takers.

stage 0 or startup

Next we start the market offering. We start offering to the public takers.

stage 1 or initial Growth

Next is the initial market growth. Here we try to get market share.

stage 2 or expand

Next is the market expansion. Here we try and increase our market size.

stage 3 or overgrowth

Next is the market capture. Here we try and become the market leader and hence no more expansion.

stage 4 or exit

Next is exit. Once we have overgrown we need to exit to stay in the business. Exit does not mean we leave the market altogether. What it means is that we must sell out or expand to other ventures in order to stay alive but unfortunately for us entrepreneurs' exit is taboo and we never plan for it.

In the next chapter we will explore the challenges facing us as entrepreneurs.

Chapter 2

Entrepreneurial Response to Challenge

"Many of life's failures are people who did not realize how close they were to success when they gave up."

Thomas A. Edison, (1847–1931)
US Inventor

Before starting this chapter, I was looking for a quote to add at the start of this chapter. The first thing that came to my mind was Google. Without hesitation, as always, I popped open my Internet Explorer and typed "QUOTE" and wow the search results were in my finger tips within two seconds and right at the top of the search results was http://www.quotationspage.com/.

You guessed it right. Yes, I pointed my mouse cursor on that and got there. This is a site full of quotes of famous people. At first I found a listing of what was going on that week and it showed Dr. Martin Luther King Jr. day. This week was also the week the first African-American President was sworn in. So I thought to myself, let me take a look at Dr. King's quotes but could not find anything suitable for this chapter. Then I wondered who would be suitable and the Mahatma (Gandhi) came to mind. Before I could go to that page Thomas Alva Edison came to my mind in rapid succession. The reason was I remembered his interview after the discovery of the light bulb where he was supposed to have said to the reporter who asked "How do you feel when you failed 2000 times?" and his response was supposed to have been one of this. I do not know if this is a true story or not but it is worthy of our attention "I found 2000 ways not to invent a light bulb" or "There are 2000 steps to a light bulb". Both responses are what we entrepreneurs would give POSITIVELY. Hence I searched for his quotes and came up with the one for this chapter.

Edison is absolutely right. Most of us fail because we do not know how near we are to success and being an entrepreneur that is the challenge YOU and I face everyday of our lives. This keeps the ENTREPRENEUR'S spirit alive. Now let us explore some of the challenges facing us entrepreneurs which we need to meet.

When I started my ventures following were some of the challenges I faced:

1. Administration and regulatory requirements

Having worked in the UK and Malaysia for five years after completing my Engineering degree, I felt it was time to take the plunge into entrepreneurship. I started off with a computer store in Ipoh, Malaysia and a web hosting venture. Till that time I had no experience whatsoever in administration or regulatory requirements as all these were always taken care of by others for me, during these five years. I had to find out many of these things and I found out the hard way that many things were not what I had thought them to be. But I had no choice except to go ahead with the venture as I had already quit my job. I found some people who worked for my father to support us in terms of administration. In terms of regulations, I discovered that the laws were not enforced as many stores were committing piracy and the authorities had no resources to control each and every one of them. But we stuck to it and refused to use pirated software.

These challenges can be met by getting training, getting help from various associations, hiring or partnering others, getting representation and/or lobbying on behalf of entrepreneurs.

2. startup Financing

For the first time in my life, I had to worry about funding my work unlike before when I had always got funding from the companies where I was working. Fortunately, I had some savings and my dear wife kindly agreed to let me use our savings for the business. Additionally, my parents also gave me a top up funding which I used to raise an overdraft facility from the bank.

These challenges can be met by looking for grants to business start ups, applying for loans specifically aimed at entrepreneurs and low cost start up loans, looking for tax concessions, equity funding and accessing loan guarantors.

3. Lack of marketing and sales skills

Being an engineer, I had no clue as to how difficult it was to market or sell our products and services. Initially, I had relied on my personal contacts and was able to make good but these soon ran out and I was not able to keep up sales. To this end, a competitor, Mr Goh, who became a good friend of mine advised me how to go about getting a ministry of finance license which would help me do some sales. We managed to do some sales but this also proved to be difficult as we did not have the skills in this area. We tried to hire people to supplement this area.

These challenges can be met by attending training, going to advice or counseling services, getting partners or hiring others to help you.

4. Growth Financing

This was again a huge task. We went to the bank and looked for more funding.

This challenge can be met as stated in point 2.

5. Lack of management skills

This was the task of having to tell people what to do. This was not easy as we worked in an environment which was small, with little profit and limited funds and so people tended to leave quickly. In this area I started to read books and chat with other entrepreneurs to get their inside story.

This challenge can be met as stated in point 3.

6. Lack of business support

We found that we lacked business support. This was due to the costs involved. We were not able to build the support around as we lacked funding. So we had to use what was available.

This challenge can be met by getting help from government bodies or trade associations.

7. Market Access

Being new entrepreneurs, we lacked market access. So we had to attend shows, seminars and supplier events to get market access.

This challenge can be met by going on trade missions with government and trade associations, attend trade shows, attend networking meetings or join business associations.

8. Protecting the idea

This was an area alien to us but fortunately regarding the store we need not know much but for the web hosting we had to learn about copyright. Cost for protecting the idea is high.

This challenge can be met by meeting costs by applying for grants to protect your idea and attending a course in this area.

9. technology access

This was another important area where we lacked and we had to learn from others.

This challenge can be met by going for new technology training, visiting trade shows and reading books and magazines.

10. Discrimination by finance providers

This happened because we were new with no track record. So we had to assure the banks that we would pay back. Here we had to rely on others' strength. We were fortunate as my parents were known to the banks, so we were extended credit based on their records.

This challenge can be met by having a good team, showing your commitment by putting some of your own money and not to taking a high salary.

11. Adapting to standards and quality

This is an area which many entrepreneurs neglect. I guess the reason is we are not aware of the standards and because we are in a hurry to make money we tend to compromise on quality. Let me caution you. This is an area YOU should NOT compromise.

This challenge can be met by learning the standards, getting Partner who might be willing to pay to obtain the standard or partner with someone who has the standards.

12. Discrimination by support providers

This again happens due to lack of a track record.

This challenge can be met as stated in point 10.

13. Lack of information

This is something for which we have no excuse. With the internet, information is on our finger tips. So please do not make this mistake. Use the internet. It is of great value for anyone.

This challenge can be met by using the internet and other information services.

These are the challenges I have come across. I hope you will be able to avoid these, to further assist you in your quest for success.

Top 75 challenges faced by other entrepreneurs listed by the National Federation of Independent Business (NFIB) in the USA which you may or may not come across but at least you will have a headstart.

1. Cost of Health Insurance
2. Cost of Natural Gas, Propane, Gasoline, Diesel, Fuel Oil
3. Federal Taxes on Business Income
4. Property Taxes (Real, Inventory or Personal Property)
5. Tax Complexity
6. Unreasonable Government Regulations
7. State Taxes on Business Income
8. Cost of Supplies / Inventories
9. Electricity Costs (Rates)
10. Workers' Compensation Costs
11. Cash Flow
12. Locating Qualified Workers
13. Cost and Availability of Liability Insurance
14. Poor Earnings (Profits)
15. Frequent Changes in Federal Tax Laws and Rules
16. Very High Fixed Costs
17. Finding and Keeping Skilled Employees
18. Federal Paperwork

19. FICA (Social Security Taxes)
20. Projecting Future Sales Changes
21. State / Local Paperwork
22. Highly Variable Earnings (Profits)
23. Controlling My Own Time
24. Telephone Costs and Service
25. Cost of Outside Business Services, e.g., Accountants, Lawyers, Consultants
26. Unemployment Compensation
27. Dealing With IRS / State Tax Agencies
28. Ability to Cost-Effectively Advertise
29. Competition From Large Businesses
30. Pricing My Goods / Services
31. Reducing Energy Use in a Cost-Effective Manner
32. Interest Rates
33. Physical Facilities Costs such as Rent / Mortgage / Maintenance
34. Death (Estate) Taxes
35. Poor Sales
36. Locating Business Help When Needed
37. Applications for Licenses, Permits, etc.
38. Finding Out About Regulatory Requirements
39. Cost of Government Required Equipment / Procedures
40. Health / Safety Regulations
41. Training Employees
42. Hiring / Firing / Employment Regulations
43. Sales Too Dependent on Health of One Business or Industry
44. Keeping Up on Business and Market Developments
45. Delinquent Accounts / Customer Financing
46. Frequency of Tax Withholding Deposits
47. Environmental Regulations
48. Using Computer(s), the Internet or New Technology Effectively
49. Handling Business Growth
50. Getting Information on Government Business Assistance Programs
51. Employee Turnover

52. Rules on Retirement Plans
53. Minimum Wage / "Living" Wage
54. Zoning / Land Use Regulations
55. Aging Workforce
56. Bad Debts (Not Delinquencies) and / or Bankruptcies
57. Crime, Including Identity Theft, Shoplifting, etc.
58. Traffic, Congestion, Parking, Highways
59. Anti-Competitive Practices, e.g., Price Fixing
60. Mandatory Family or Sick Leave
61. Getting Useful Business Information
62. Protecting Intellectual Property
63. False Insurance Claims, Such as for Workers' Comp and UC
64. Solid and Hazardous Waste Disposal
65. Costs and Frequency of Law Suits / Threatened Suits
66. Competition From Imported Products
67. Credit Rating / Record Errors
68. Increased National Security Requirements
69. Competition From Internet Businesses
70. Undocumented Workers (Illegal Aliens)
71. Winning Contracts From Federal / State / Local Governments
72. Obtaining Short-Term (Less Than 12 Months or Revolving) Business Loans
73. Obtaining Long-Term (5 Years or More) Business Loans
74. Access to High-Speed Internet
75. Exporting My Products / Services

Now that we have taken a look at the challenges let us move on. What next? Do you want to be an entrepreneur? I said in the first chapter to SAY NO – WHY? Because that is the hardest thing you will ever have to do to be an entrepreneur. Try saying NO. Was that hard? NO? so say YES!

Now what!

I am now going to show you a process involving eight steps which needs to be taken for being a GREAT entrepreneur.

1. Come up with an idea
2. Carry out a study
3. Form the team

4. Start the venture
5. Get a business plan together
6. Look for interested investors
7. Grow the idea
8. Prepare for exit

In the next chapter, I will discuss "how to generate an idea and determine the opportunity".

Entrepreneurs' Tools to Determine Ideas

"It is no use saying, 'We are doing our best.' You have got to succeed in doing what is necessary."

Sir Winston Churchill, (1874–1965)
British politician

"Reveal your ideas to others and be proud of them."

Muthu Singaram, 2005

Most sources of ideas come from technical or market requirement by universities, companies and individuals. Contrary to belief, we often hear from our participants and students that they want to be entrepreneurs but to our surprise their response is "we do not have an idea and do not know how to get one." You can get an idea by using the many tools available to you. There are many techniques available to you. We will explore 25 of these in this book.

interviewing

In interviewing we need one facilitator and carefully selected six to twelve people. This should be a discussion and not just asking questions about products to fulfill the market needs. The session should last half-a-day and a token sum or reward should be given to the participants for their time. This method can be used not only to generate ideas but can be used to screen ideas and concepts.

classical brainstorming

In classical brainstorming, we start with a problem statement. The statement should not be too broad or narrow. We need one facilitator and carefully selected six to twelve people. Here, we must have a free flow discussion to generate more ideas. Each and every idea generated must be recorded (most of the ideas will not materialize). Then we should combine all ideas and come up with one or two ideas which we can work on. During this session, criticism and negative remarks are not allowed. The session should have a time limit like half-a-day or a full day.

negative brainstorming

This is somewhat similar to classical brainstorming. But during this session criticism and negative remarks are allowed but you must ensure no personal attacks or demoralization of the group members take place. The purpose of this session is to knock an idea down. This is a good technique to be used before using the other techniques as the group will be aware of what problems they are to overcome.

rawlinson brainstorming

Again, this is somewhat similar to classical brainstorming. However, during this session, all feedback is directed to the facilitator and not to the group. This is a good technique if there are enough people to capture and note down all the ideas.

This is a good technique for new groups.

Value brainstorming

Yet again, this is somewhat similar to classical brainstorming. Here, we list the primary concern and hidden values that lie behind the primary concern. Then we rank the hidden values and define what each means and arrive at an idea.

Then put into action the ranked results.

collective note book (cnb)

Facilitator provides a note book to all team members with a problem statement. The note book will contain some suggestions to help generate ideas. For a month everyone writes one idea everyday in the note book. Facilitator will provide regular related information during the month. At the end of the month each member presents summary of their ideas in brief. At the end of the month the facilitator collects the note books and consolidates the ideas.

Then all the members will view the note books and the facilitator's comments on them to come up with the final idea.

Factors in 'selling' ideas

This method is used when selling an idea with context and content. We need to differentiate and define context and content for this method to work. In terms of context we must have timing, right audience and an idea owner. In terms of content, we should use simple language and stress key points but must be clear in our statement and provide evidence to show the need for the idea. We must have a list of both advantages and disadvantages and be prepared to take questions. No idea is flawless.

False Faces

Here, we need to define the problem statement and make assumptions. These must be challenged, reversed and we must write the opposite for each assumption. We need to record as many viewpoints and ideas as possible that might be produced in each reversal.

Fishbone diagram

This is a great tool used in manufacturing to solve issues related during manufacturing. This is also known as Ishikawa diagram named after the original developer and is also known as the cause and effect diagram. By using a fishbone we can identify solution for issues, that is, we can generate ideas. This is done over a number of sittings to allow the team members to get involved. First, a main fishbone is arrived at, then each team will take smaller bones and look for solution which will form the basis of the idea.

Five W's and h

This is popular in the world of journalism. When a journalist is looking for a story they always ask Who? Why? What? Where? When? How? This can be applied easier to generate an idea.

Why?

Repeatedly asking "why" questions enables us to arrive at a solution. The reason for this is we get frustrated by the repeated whys so we arrive at a solution. Great tool to get information from anyone. Try it!

Free Association

Here we combine several idea techniques together. There are two ways to start one, a serial start with a trigger and record all the ideas which flow or the other centered similar to classical brainstorming where you have multiple ideas. This is a good method for a more experienced team as you would have done idea generation using several different methods already.

Forced relationships

Here we try and force relationships between products to generate a new product. We need to isolate the elements of the problem and then define, record, and analyse the relationship between these elements to reach a new idea.

Fresh eye and networking

This method is usually used after we identify an idea. We get people who are not involved with the original idea generation for their suggestions. With their inputs we then improve the idea. We must provide feedback to the people who took part so they are aware what we have done with their inputs. This is a wonderful method to improve and validate an idea which we have generated.

Goal orientation

This is often a popular method in companies as it puts pressure on people to come up with ideas. Here the company or the company's representative would set a goal and we will then try and list the ideas that we come up with. Then we would list the needs, difficulties and the external constraints in executing these ideas. Once we have done this, we will then write the problem statement.

Attribute listing (and variants)

This is done by taking an existing product and breaking it into parts and identifying solutions to achieve these parts. This is somewhat like doing reverse engineering. We then recombine these solutions to arrive at a new product.

creative problem solving (cPs)

This is a method, popular now, with innovation written all over the place. Here we search for issues, collect data and then convert the narrow statement into a broad statement and then generate ideas. After this we find a solution for the issues and accept the solution.

critical path diagrams (cPD)

This is an engineering tool where we use path diagrams. Here we would list all the actives and sub actives along with start and finish dates and then construct the diagram. Then we check the diagram, calculate the earliest and latest dates for each activity and adjust as required, arriving at the solution.

heuristic ideation technique (hit)

Here we select two items of interest and make a list of each component of these items. Once this is done, a contract matrix is generated. Then we would cross out what is existing and identify a cell which has market potential. Once this is done, we look at the matrix from another angle.

Then make the cells into workable ideas. HIT has 3 rules of thumb (i) new ideas are a combination of existing ones, (ii) they can be defined by two elements and (iii) the combination of dissimilar items work better than similar items.

Keeping a dream diary

Before we sleep we will tell ourselves several times that we will not forget our dreams when we get up. We also need to fill our mind with activities which will generate these dreams. When we wake up we need to lie quietly with our eyes closed and try and remember our dream. We need a notebook next to us to record these dreams and we cannot miss a single day until we reach an idea.

Morphological analysis

This is an extension of Attribute Listing. When you look at the new ideas you will find some are impossible to execute and some already exist. So you have to remove all these and you will be left with several new ideas which you can choose from.

Plan Do check Act (PDcA)

This is another engineering tool that engineers use to run their projects. **Plan**: Identify the opportunity then come up with a solution. **Do**: Test the solution. **Check**: See if the outcome is desirable **Act:** If it is a desirable result, accept the solution if not start again with the knowledge you have gained.

relaxation

Relaxing is not only good for anxiety alleviation but also useful in idea generation. We can recite a script to relax ourselves. If you do not have a script you can recite a prayer or a poem. Most people, unless they are relaxed, will not be able to come up with new ideas. So this is a good method.

strategic management process

This is the famous management consultant tool. We collect historical context and carry out a situational analysis i.e. SWOT and STEP. This will result in the issues. We then look for solutions and see if they are feasible. If feasible, we implement the idea.

Anonymous voting

This is a great method to help people to talk. Start with a list of ideas identified. The facilitator then tells the members to make a short list by telling them how many ideas to select. Members select the ideas and list them serially. From here an idea is selected. This is good for people who are shy and quiet.

Now that we have examined 25 methods it is worth noting that these techniques are from different areas i.e. Journalism, Engineering, Management and others. It shows that all of us rely on idea generation to execute our work. Your attention must have been drawn to the fact that you might need to use several methods together to generate your idea. You select a technique which is suitable to you and your team and apply that technique.

Now that we know how to generate an idea we need to determine the opportunity for the idea. Ideas are not opportunities but they are merely a tool for opportunity. An idea becomes an opportunity only if there is a need or a want. The idea must be based on a solution and must be market-driven. We need to identify the stakeholders and create value for them.

There are two approaches to determine opportunity (i) The Systematic approach (by late Professor Peter Drucker) and (ii) The Market approach.

DeterMininG by systeMAtic APProAch

unexpected

- This is probably the largest source. This happens unexpectedly and it can come from unexpected success, unexpected failure or unexpected outside events.

incongruities

- This is a discrepancy between what it is and what it ought to be. This is basically a fault leading to opportunity.

Process need

- This is a necessity and an opportunity results from this.

industry and Market structures

- This happens when there is a need for change in an industry or market structure.

Demographics

- This happens due to change in population in terms of size, age, composition, education, income etc.

change in Perception

- This happens when we look at things differently and gives rise to an opportunity.

new Knowledge

- This is the big one and gets a lot of limelight and creates history.

We have not gone into the details as you can read Professor Peter Drucker's book *Innovation and Entrepreneurship* to get the full details.

DeterMininG by MArKet APProAch

step 1

How do these products create value for a potential customer? Do these products offer improvements or lower cost for the customer? Next, what are the barriers to adopt these products? Are these considered barriers because they are not user friendly? If yes, do they need training? Is the market slow to adopt new products? Do adopting these new products make other products obsolete? We now need to find out how to overcome these barriers. Once we have overcome these barriers then we conclude two things— the potential demand and the revenue.

step 2

Next we need to look at what are the risks. The risks will fall under three areas technical risks, financial risks and competitive risks. In terms of technical risks, we must see to it that the product is not easy to duplicate otherwise it would be easy entry for others. The financial risk should be taken into account if the investment can be recovered from the venture. The competitor risk is always there. The only time when, there is no competition is (1) when no one has seen the opportunity and (2) when there is no opportunity.

step 3

If our idea leads to a product, we analyse the production and manufacturing process. The question we need to ask is "can we produce at the right cost sufficient numbers of the product?"

step 4

This is a very important step; if we are not able to handle the initial cost to setup then having just an idea is of no use.

step 5

Here we must expand the risks determined in step 2.

The unfortunate thing about us entrepreneurs is that we tend to fall in love with our ideas and ignore the billion dollar question "does it have an opportunity". This leads us to say that people do not fail but only ideas fail, because they did not have an opportunity in the first place. Now that this has been brought to light and the approach has been clearly explained to you, we hope you will focus on this aspect of entrepreneurship very seriously, to ensure success for your ideas.

In the next chapter, we will explore the entrepreneur's vehicle to success. There are two components, the first is to form a team and the second is to have a legal entity.

Chapter 4

Entrepreneurial Vehicle for Success

"A great team can make a world of difference to a mediocre idea."

Muthu Singaram, 2005

Now that you have determined the opportunity, you have to make good use of this wonderful opportunity. You cannot do it yourself. You need a vehicle to achieve this. There are two components which are equally important for the success of the opportunity. The first is the formation of a team and the second is for this team to have a legal entity.

ForMAtion oF A teAM

Let me draw your attention here to the fact that team formation is totally different from team building and team work. The first step is formation of a team, then building it and then team work.

There are many team theories but in this book we will explore the most successful theory which in my humble opinion is "Tuckman's Stages". This theory was developed by Bruce Tuckman, an American psychologist in 1965 with four stages and added a fifth stage in 1977.

Before we explore this theory let me emphasize the following points. The team will drive a venture forward more than the product or services. The team will transform a creative idea into a commercially viable idea. Venture Capitals prefer a first class team with a second class idea. This team needs a leader just like every ship needs a captain. The team also needs a legal entity.

When forming a team you should ask the following questions first. What tasks need to be completed by the team? To complete these tasks effectively what skills does the team need? What, exactly, does this team need to do to complete these tasks? Who has the necessary skills and how long will it take to complete the task? What are checks and balances for the team to know when the task is completed and how will the team measure the ongoing progress? How will the team recognize and reward team members? How will the team actively exploit individual ideas and skills?

Bruce Tuckman's original model had four stages *Forming, Storming, Norming, Performing* and he later added a fifth stage *Adjourning*.

stage 1: Forming

During the forming stage the team is highly dependent on the leader for guidance and direction. The team would not be much in agreement on team goals other than those received from its leader. The team members would be uncertain and unclear on individual roles and responsibilities so this needs to be defined. The leader must be prepared to handle lots of questions about the team's purpose, objectives and external relationships. During this stage the leadership style is likely to be the "tells" type.

We need to allow time for team members to get acquainted. The team must review its purpose and goals, and share individual goals. The team should share strengths and challenges related to working on teams. It must create initial guidelines for working together as a team. It must determine task-related details and develop team communication and conflict management skills proactively. The team conducts a group check-in at the end of meetings and provide active task and process leadership.

stage 2: storming

During the storming stage the team will have lots of contesting and debating on team decisions. Team members will be seeking positions by attempting to establish themselves in relation to other team members and the leader. The leader may receive challenges from the team members to become the leader. Their aims will become more defined but uncertainty will still exist. There are possibilities at this stage for cliques and factions to be formed and there may be power struggles. During this stage the leadership is likely to have moved to a more "sells" type.

The team needs to promote open a constructive communication. It must allow conflicts but must be able to manage conflicts collaboratively. The team should focus on short-term goals by encouraging a positive and supportive atmosphere. The team must provide empowering leadership.

stage 3: norming

During the norming stage the team stays to agreement and consensus tends to have been reached, with minor disagreements. Now the roles and responsibilities should be defined and accepted by the team. Major decisions are made collectively by group agreement but minor decisions may be delegated to individuals or small teams within a group. The team discusses and develops its working "guidelines", processes and working style.

The team must maintain open communication. By doing this, the team will increase focus on performance goals. It must acknowledge team members and celebrate team achievements. Encourage shared leadership.

stage 4: Performing

During the performing stage the team is clear about its functions. The team has a shared knowledge and understanding and requires little inputs from the leader. The team starts to focus on achieving goals and makes the most of the decisions based on agreed criteria with the leader. Disagreements still occur, but now they are resolved positively by the team. Team members look after each other and share common "bond" and group individuality.

The team must encourage innovation and conduct periodical team assessments. The team must\continue to acknowledge and celebrate successes. Share team leadership roles.

This theory was amended by the original theorist (Bruce Tuckman) and a fifth stage called Adjourning, which is also referred to as Deforming and Mourning was added.

stage 5: Adjourning

During the adjourning stage the team breaks up. Hopefully the project is fulfilled at this stage. The team can move on to new things, feeling good about what's been achieved.

From an organisational perspective, there should be recognition and sensitivity to people's vulnerabilities, particularly if members of the group have been closely bonded and feel a sense of insecurity or threat from this change. Feelings of insecurity would be natural for people with high 'steadiness' attributes.

Adjourning is arguably more of an adjunct to the original four stage model rather than an extension. It views the group from a perspective beyond the purpose of the first four stages.

The Adjourning phase is certainly very relevant to the people in the group and their well-being, but not to the main task of managing and developing a team, which is clearly central to the original four stages.

business As A LeGAL entity

What is A business?

Business is an activity in which one provides goods or services at a profit. Every business is carried on with this intention such as trade, commerce, craftsmanship and professions.

types of business

In India, a business may be carried on in any one of the following forms — Sole Proprietorships, Partnerships, Joint Stock Companies as Private Limited Company or Public Limited Company, Cooperative and Joint Hindu Family Firm.

sole Proprietorships

This is the easiest, simplest and oldest form. The business is owned and controlled by an individual and it has no separate legal entity. Hence it has unlimited liability, undivided risk, individual funding and in India there is no need to register it.

Partnerships

Partnerships are formed by two or more people (maximum 10 people in banking and 20 people in non-banking). The formation is done by an agreement known as Partnership Deed. The activity must be lawful business and the profits shared with unlimited liability. The parties are restricted on transfer of interest and based on utmost good faith. The partnership can be dissolved by a number of means and registration is optional.

Joint Stock Companies

There are two types of companies— private and public.

Private

To form a private limited company, you need minimum two members and maximum 50 members. The company, name must be ABC Private Limited with minimum two directors and can't invite public to buy shares. It must be registered and its liability limited.

Public

To form a public limited company you need minimum seven and there is no maximum number. The company name must be ABC Limited with minimum three directors and can invite public to buy shares. It must be registered and liability limited.

Cooperative

A cooperative is formed by a group of people who join voluntarily to improve their economic interests. Cooperatives often share their earnings by dividing the profits among its members in the form of dividends.

Joint Hindu Family Firm

A Hindu Joint Family or Hindu United family (HUF) or a Joint Hindu Family is an extended family arrangement among Hindus in India, comprising of many generations, living under the same roof. The male members are blood relatives and all the women are either mothers, wives, unmarried daughters, or widowed relatives. In Hindu society it is common for families to carry not only family duties together but also all other activities. The family is headed usually by the oldest male, who makes decisions on economic and social matters on behalf of the entire family. His wife generally controls the kitchen, children upbringing and religious activities. All income goes to a common pool and is shared by the members. These types of firms are on the decline but we have mentioned this just for your information.

Which structure is riGht For you?

	Sole Prop	Partnership	Company	Cooperative
Professionals	X	X		
Foreign Partners			X	
No legal issues facing the business	X	X		
Potential legal issues facing the business			X	
For outside finance			X	
For quick Decisions	X			
For common Benefit				X

In short, there are four major types of structures that most small entrepreneurs can consider. These are Sole Proprietorship, Partnership, Companies and Cooperatives. Based on the table of comparison each type has its pros and cons. You must choose carefully as to which structure is suitable for you now and in the future. You need to know your rights and desired role of the company.

Once you have decided as to which structure is suitable for you, the next step is to arrive at a name. Believe it or not, there are two schools of thoughts here— one says the name makes a difference and the other says no. I leave this decision to you.

It is interesting to take a look at how some companies got their names. I cannot say for sure that this information is accurate but nevertheless it is useful for us to think about this.

- **Adobe**: It came from the name of the river Adobe Creek that ran behind the house of founder John Warnock.
- **Apache**: It got its name because its founders got started by applying patches to code written for NCSA's http? daemon. The result was 'A PAtCHy' server -- thus, the name Apache.
- **Jakarta:** (project from Apache) - A project constituted by SUN and Apache to create a web server handling servlets and JSPs. Jakarta was the name of the conference room at SUN where most of the meetings between SUN and Apache took place.
- **Tomcat**: The servlet part of the Jakarta project. Tomcat was the code-name for the JSDK 2.1 project inside SUN.
- **Apple Computers**: the favourite fruit of founder, Steve Jobs. He was three months late in filing a name for the business, and he threatened to call his company Apple Computers if the other colleagues didn't suggest a better name by 5 o'clock.
- **C**: Dennis Ritchie improved on the B programming language and called it 'New B'. He later called it C. Earlier B was created by Ken Thompson as a revision of the Bon programming language (named after his wife Bonnie).
- **C++**: Bjarne Stroustrup called his new language 'C with Classes' and then new C' because of which the original C began to be called 'old C' which was considered insulting to the C community. At this time Rick Mascitti suggested the name C++ as a successor to C.
- **CISCO**: It is not an acronym but the short name for San Francisco.
- **Compaq**: Using COMp, for computer, and PAQ to denote a small integral object.
- **Corel**: From the founder's name Dr. Michael Cowpland. It stands for COwpland REsearch Laboratory.
- **GNU**: A species of African antelope. Founder of the GNU project Richard Stallman liked the name because of the humour associated with its pronunciation and was also influenced by the children's song 'The Gnu Song' which is a song sung by a gnu. Also it fitted into the recursive acronym culture with 'GNU's Not Unix'.
- **Google**: The name started as a joke and boasts about the amount of information the search-engine would be able to search. It was originally named 'Googol', a word

for the number represented by 1 followed by 100 zeros. After founders, Stanford graduate students Sergey Brin and Larry Page presented their project to an Angel investor, they received a cheque made out to 'Google' !

- **HCL**: Hindustan Computers Ltd. started by Shiv Nadar.
- **Hotmail**: Founder Jack Smith got the idea of accessing e-mail via the web from a computer anywhere in the world. When Sabeer Bhatia came up with the business plan for the mail service, he tried all kinds of names ending in 'mail' and finally settled for hotmail as it included the letters "html" -the programming language that is used to write web pages. It was initially referred to as HoTMaiL with selective upper casing.
- **HP**: Bill Hewlett and Dave Packard tossed a coin to decide whether the company they founded would be called Hewlett-Packard or Packard-Hewlett.
- **Intel:** Bob Noyce and Gordon Moore wanted to name their new company 'Moore Noyce' but that was already trademarked by a hotel chain, so they had to settle for an acronym of INTegrated ELectronics.
- **Java**: Originally called Oak by creator James Gosling, from the tree that stood outside his window, the programming team had to look for a substitute as there was another language with the same name. Java was selected from a list of suggestions. It came from the name of the coffee that the programmers drank.
- **LG:** Combination of two popular Korean brands Lucky and Goldstar.
- **Linux:** Linus Torvalds originally used the Minix OS on his system which he replaced by his OS. Hence the working name was Linux (Linus' Minix). He thought the name to be too egotistical and planned to name it Freax(free + freak + x). His friend Ari Lemmke encouraged Linus to upload it to a network so it could be easily downloaded. Ari gave Linus a directory called linux on his FTP server, as he did not like the name Freax.(Linus' parents named him after two-time Nobel Prize winner Linus Pauling).
- **Lotus** (Notes): Mitch Kapor got the name for his company from 'The Lotus Position' or 'Padmasana'. Kapor used to be a teacher of Transcendental Meditation of Maharishi Mahesh Yogi.
- **Microsoft**: Coined by Bill Gates to represent the company that was devoted to MICROcomputer SOFTware. Originally christened Micro-Soft, the '-' was removed later on.
- **Motorola:** Founder Paul Galvin came up with this name when his company started manufacturing radios for cars. The popular radio company at that time was called Victrola.
- **Mozilla**: When Marc Andreesen, founder of Netscape, created a broswer to replace Mosaic (also developed by him), it was named Mozilla (Mosaic-Killer,Godzilla). The marketing guys didn't like the name however and it was re-christened Netscape Navigator.

- **Mercedes**: This was actually the financier's daughter's name.
- **SAP:** "Systems, Applications, Products in Data Processing", formed by 4 ex-IBM employees who used to work in the 'Systems/Applications/Projects' group of IBM.
- **ORACLE**: Larry Ellison and Bob Oats were working on a consulting project for the CIA (Central Intelligence Agency). The code name for the project was called Oracle(the CIA saw this as the system to give answers to all questions or something to that effect.). The project was designed to help use the newly written SQL code by IBM. The project was eventually terminated but Larry and Bob decided to finish what they started and bring it to the world. They kept the name Oracle and created the RDBMS engine. Later they kept the same name for the company.
- **Red Hat**: Company founder Marc Ewing was given the Cornell lacrosse team cap (with red and white stripes) while at college by his grandfather. He lost it and had to search for it desperately. The manual of the beta version of Red Hat Linux had an appeal to readers to return his Red Hat if found by anyone !
- **SCO (UNIX)**: from Santa Cruz Operation. The company's office was in Santa Cruz.
- **Sony**: from the Latin word 'sonus' meaning sound, and 'sonny' a slang used by Americans to refer to a bright youngster.
- **SUN**: founded by 4 Stanford University buddies, SUN is the acronym for Stanford University Network. Andreas Bechtolsheim built a microcomputer; Vinod Khosla recruited him and Scott McNealy to manufacture computers based on it, and Bill Joy to develop a UNIX-based OS for the computer.
- **UNIX**: When Bell Labs pulled out of MULTICS (MULTiplexed Information and Computing System), which was originally a joint Bell/GE/MIT project, Ken Thompson and Dennis Ritchie of Bell Labs wrote a simpler version of the OS. They needed the OS to run the game Space War which was compiled under MULTICS. It was called UNICS - UNIplexed operating and Computing System by Brian Kernighan. It was later shortened to UNIX.
- **Xerox:** The inventor, Chestor Carlson, named his product trying to say 'dry' (as it was dry copying, markedly different from the then prevailing wet copying). The Greek root `xer' means dry.
- **Yahoo!**: The word was invented by Jonathan Swift and used in his book *Gulliver's Travels*. It represents a person who is repulsive in appearance and action and is barely human. Yahoo! founders Jerry Yang and David Filo selected the name because they considered themselves yahoos.
- **3M**: Minnesota Mining and Manufacturing Company started off by mining the material corundum used to make sandpaper.

Now that we know how to get a vehicle to make good the opportunitiy, let us go to the next chapter to see how we can protect our idea.

Part ii

Entrepreneurial Flourish: Getting a Financial Grip

Chapter 5
Source of Funding and Support

"I don't know the key to success, but the key to failure is trying to please everybody."

Bill Cosby (1937–)
US comedian and television actor

Now that we have explored how to protect our own idea, we need to make it a reality. In order to do so we need funding. In this chapter we will explore how you can go about funding your 7idea. I love the quote at the start of this chapter by Josephine Tessier and I absolutely agree with her and I am sure you will agree too.

There are many ways to get funding. Before we go into that let us review the "MONEY RULE".

Money Rule

Those with it make the rules. Money is there but you need to know where to seek it. To be successful you must be able to successfully raise funds. Money for your ideas are "risk money" to the stakeholder.

Why Do you neeD FunDinG?

The reason why you usually need funding is for

- Fixed capital (this will include equipment, fixed assets),
- Working capital (this will include rental, salaries and other day-to-day expenses) and
- Growth capital (this will be for expansion).

sources oF FunDinG

There are several sources of fund available to you. The most common ones are:

- Personal savings
- Friends and family
- Venture capital
- Angels and private investors

- Corporations
- Grants and Incentives i.e. State, Federal and Agencies
- Debt financing
- Initial public offering (IPO)

Besides personal savings the others are sometimes refered to as OPM (pronounced as opium) Other Peoples Money. Contrary to the belief, actually it is harder to manage OPM than your own money. Now let us take a look at each one of these sources.

Personal savings

Most entrepreneurs usually start off their business with their personal savings as this would be the easiest source of funding. However, if you are a young person, you will most likely not have a large amount of savings. Even other funders prefer to fund entrepreneurs who have invested some of their own money, as this will give confidence to the investor that the entrepreneur is serious about his venture. However, it is difficult to continue funding with your funds. So at some time you will need to look for other funds.

Friends and family

Next line of funding can usually be raised from friends and family. This you will need to return and in the event you are NOT able to return, this can create unnecessary tension and lead to other issues. This is particularly true in Asian culture.

Venture capital

These are companies which invest for equity in your company. So in the event if you do not make it you do not need to return the funds but these people will usually take an active role in your company. We are going to spend sometime on this and understand how this works.

Venture capital is a term to describe financing for startups and early stage businesses as well as businesses in "turnaround" situations. Venture capital investments are usually high risk investments, but with above average returns. A Venture Capitalist (VC) is a person who makes the investments.

Venture capital funds are made up of the financial capital of third party investors that are used to fund businesses which are considered too risky for typical equity investors or bank loans. These third parties' source of funds are known as alternative investment and come from savings accounts, insurance policies, company stocks and shares, unit trust and pension funds. The reason why some of these funds become available is because some of these venture capital investments give high returns.

The venture capital takes the form of either equity participation, or a combination of equity participation and debt obligation which are convertible debt instruments that become equity if a certain level of risk is exceeded.

The venture capitalist becomes part owner of the new venture. Most investments are structured as preferred shares and the common stock often reserved by covenant for a future buyout, as VC investment criteria usually include a planned exit event (an IPO or acquisition), normally within three to seven years.

Role of the venture capitalist

- To provide funds for high risk but high return ventures.
- To arrange additional financing from other sources if required.
- To constantly assist study and revise the proposed business model and work on reformulating the overall strategy.
- To be on the look out for identifying and employing key people and firing.
- To provide help in identifying supportive service companies and other business contacts.
- To help buying-out existing partners (owners) where they think this is necessary.
- To provide operational and technical guidance to enhance overall business efficiency.
- To prepare the company for a potential exit (e.g. acquisition or initial public offering).

Types of venture capital

- Seed funding is usually given for marketing research, concept testing, alpha and beta testing.
- Startup funding is given to get started.
- Second-stage funding is given to expand to the next level.
- Mezzanine financing is given to bail out troubled companies with huge potential and is usually given as debt funding but to be converted to equity at a later date.

What is the benefit to the VC?

Limited partners usually offer these funds. The people who manage are general partners. They are paid a management fee (1.5 to 3%) of the fund and a profit sharing (20 to 30 %). The fund life is eight to ten years and because of this the exit is around three to seven years. VCs add value to your company and that is the reason why you must do research on VCs first.

Large VC funds do not mean that these VCs will invest in new ventures. Many established VCs sometimes avoid new startups and concentrate on shorter exit. Exit is by IPO, selling to others, management buyout and merger. Out of 10 ventures, one will give huge returns, two will give good returns, 3 will return investment and four will give no returns. VCs are looking at two to 20 times gain.

How to Approach Venture Capitalists?

Step 1 Investment Criteria

Usually you can get these from their websites. Some of the investment criteria that VC are looking for, are, strong management team, differentiated product or services, a potentially large market opportunity, the barriers to entry, visibility of exit mechanism, location and size of investment.

Depending on the size of fund and success of their portfolio, they will start investing right from the early stages because the early stages require more work. Sometimes, it is worth talking to experienced fund raisers to know more.

Step 2 Going on the Road Show

When you raise funds you are selling a portion of your company. There is no need to tell about "How fantastic your service or product is" but "What it will help to." It might be worth paying an expert to raise the fund.

Step 3 Good Team

VCs invest in good teams and not the technology. They do not expect all members to be in place. A good VC helps to hire these at the right time. The team must be fully committed.

Step 4 Pitching for funds

Do not send mass e-mails. It is a selling exercise so target your audience. Find out why VCs fund. Do your homework by looking at their portfolio in terms of background, preferences, their likes and dislikes, try and get a reference i.e. accountants, lawyers etc. Get used to a "NO".

What VCs do and monitor

- VC's structure the board and shareholding outside.
- Give equity based compensation for team members.
- Provide value added service and shapes the company by playing an active role and protecting their investment.
- Limits outside involvement.
- Help in bringing your product or service to the market in a shorter time. They fire the founder CEOs and hire new ones if necessary and this they do it professionally. They hire via professional channels and then through informal channels. They play a supportive role and link up small companies with bigger ones.

What do VCs do after funding?

VCs do any one of these things:
- Go IPO and sell all the shares.
- Go IPO and sell part of the shares.
- Fund further to the next stage.
- Sell the firm.

Angels and private investors

Angels and private investors are high net worth individuals who invest on young startups. They will fund using their own funds. Besides funding, they also provide mentoring. In return, depending on your negotiation skills they will take some percentage of the venture, usually between 10 to 50 %.

corporations

Sometimes you will be able to convince a larger company to fund you. This is how corporate entrepreneurship flourishes as companies do not want to lose a good employee to entrepreneurship. By supporting and investing on these young entrepreneurs the larger company will benefit by having a new venture within the organization. Quite often, entrepreneurs think that telling their present boss that they have an idea, is not really a good idea. These entrepreneurs feel their bosses will not be happy to know that you are going to be an entrepreneur. But today, with the world changing at high speed, companies are quite willing to explore these new and bright ideas of young entrepreneurs.

Grants and incentives i.e. state, Federal and Agencies

There are several grants available at state and national level for which you can apply. Usually these grants are not repayable. However, these are reimbursements which means you need to actually spend before getting the fund from the agencies.

Debt financing

These are funding, you need to repay to the bank. The people who provide these fundings are commercial banks, assets-based lenders, trade credit, equipment suppliers, commercial finance companies, savings and loan companies, stockbrokerage firms, insurance companies and credit union.

initial Public offering (iPo)

This is when you offer the share in your company to the public and raise funds. You raise money only the first time you sell the shares after which the money is only transacted between the buyer and seller.

Which source is best For you?

Type	VC	Angel	Family	Self	Loans	Grants	IPO
Small Amount		X	X	X			
Large Amount	X						
Long time to profit	X	X	X			X	
Short time to profit		X	X	X	X		
NPO						X	
Expansion	X						
New Technology	X	X					
Proven Technology	X	X	X		X		X

The above table gives a quick look at the criteria of each fund and will help you decide the fund suitable for your venture.

hoW to Get heLP?

In India there are state and central agencies which provide help to entrepreneurs. These are some of the agencies which provide help in India. The list has been compiled from different sources for you to know that there are many agencies in India.

Agencies / Institutional Support

- District Industries Centres
- Small Industries Development Corporation
- National Small Industries Corporation Limited
- Directorates of Industries of The State Governments
- State Small Industries Corporations
- Entrepreneurial Guidance Bureau
- National Alliance of Young Entrepreneurs
- Small Industry Extension Training Institute
- National Productivity Council
- National Research Development Corporation of India
- Khadi and Village Industries Commission
- Technical Consultancy Organisations
- Industrial and Technical Consultancy Organisation of Tamilnadu
- Specialised Institutions
  - National Institute of Entrepreneurship and Small Business Development
  - National Institute of Small Industries Extension Training
- Central Institute of Tool Design
- Central Tool Room Training Centres
- Industrial Estates
- Commercial Banks

Now that we have explored how to get funding and help, we need to know how much funding, what are we going to use the fund for and how are we going to use them. In the next chapter we will look at financial management.

Chapter 6

Basic Accounting

"The company exists to make money. The goal of a manufacturing organization is to make money."

Eliyahu M.Goldratt (1947–2011)
– Physicist & Management Guru

As I must acknowledge here the next four chapters has been written by my friend Professor S. Srikanth. Before we really take the plunge, let us go through some fundamental concepts of finance and business.

soMe FunDAMentAL concePts

economic Activity

Economic activity is that which is carried on with the purpose of getting an economic reward. An activity, however small but involving give and take of 'money', can be simply defined as an economic activity.

A large number of economic activities continuously take place in any business, e.g., hiring premises on rent is an economic activity. Hiring a workman for wages, purchasing of raw material or selling of any goods and services are economic activities.

business

Business consists of a number of economic activities which are carried on with the ultimate purpose of generation of profits. The input for business (again for common understanding) is 'money' and the output is also 'money'; only the output of money should preferably be more than the input.

the Finance Function

The finance function on an overall basis is related to the raising of 'resources' and aiding and ensuring proper use of these 'resources'. 'Resources' really is a very wide concept and so, for simple understanding we can say 'money'.

What is Profit?

To put it very simply, profit is the excess of income over expense,

i.e. Profit = Income – Expenses.

the need for Accounting

The next question is how are profits determined? Well, it is not as simple, as the formula

Profit = Income – Expenses

You need to visualise how many activities and transactions take place in the business. To arrive at the profit, it will be necessary to record all such transactions in a proper and systematic manner and then work on these figures. This is where the need for recording transactions or the need for accounting comes up.

Accounting is a systematic method of recording monetary transactions.

Any transaction that affects the entity in specific monetary terms is an Accounting Transaction. An accountable transaction is the basic unit of business.

AccountinG – the systeMAtic WAy

We have seen that recording of transactions is required to arrive at the profit of a business. It is also clear that this recording has to be done in a systematic manner. Over the years, universally accepted accounting principles and practices have evolved and today we are in a situation where in most of the world, the basic accounting principles are accepted uniformly.

The entire structure of accounting rests on the foundation of certain concepts. We will look at some of the most important concepts or principles:

1) The Dual Aspect Concept
2) The Going Concern Concept
3) The Business Entity Concept

The first principle, i.e. The Dual Aspect or Dual Transaction principle, is the starting point of what is today known as Double-Entry accounting. This will be described in detail a little later.

The second principle i.e. The Going Concern Concept, assumes that a business has been started with the idea of the business being continuously carried on and not for short periods or for only few transactions. It assumes that the business will be carried on forever.

The third principle i.e. The Business Entity Concept, emphasizes that the 'business' and the 'entrepreneur' are separate entities. The business is a separate entity absolutely distinct from the owner. In simple terms this means the owner whether proprietor, partners in the case of a firm or shareholders in the case of a limited company, are also "owed" money by the entity which has a separate accounting business entity for the purpose of accounting.

the DoubLe entry systeM (Dual Aspect concept)

We now enter the famous (or shall we say notorious!) subject of pure accounting. As a matter of interest one should know that, the earliest book on double-entry accounting system, that has been found was written by Lucas Pacioli in the 15th century. He is often called the "father of accounting".

This system of accounting is, as mentioned earlier, followed universally. This has evolved over the years to take care of the growing complexity of business.

Earlier, a single entry system of accounting was followed where all transactions were just recorded chronologically. From this system it was not possible to get a proper understanding of the affairs of the business, especially with relation to amounts receivable and payable and therefore, this system slowly got phased out. Though in small and traditional businesses this method is said to be used today, these few instances are of little relevance.

Dual Aspect of every transaction

The fundamental principle on which the Double Entry Accounting is based, is that, for every transaction there are always two aspects, e.g. if there is a receiver there must also be a giver. Let's understand this with an example:

Suppose A pays Rs.10,000 in cash to X – which are the two aspects of this transaction?

The first aspect is that X has received 'cash' of Rs.10,000. The second aspect is that X has received the cash of Rs.10,000 from A – the giver.

So when X has to record this transaction he will not only record that he has received Rs.10,000 but also that this has been received from A. This is the dual aspect of the transaction.

Look at the same transaction from Mr.A's angle. Here the first aspect is that X has received cash from A, the giver and cash has gone out of the business, since it has been paid to X.

Similarly, all transactions in a business will have a dual aspect and under the Double Entry Accounting System both these aspects have to be recorded.

This principle of dual nature of transactions is absolutely fundamental and as much a reality as the fact that every coin must have two sides!

Transactions

What is the meaning of a transaction? To put it in a simple way, a transaction is any dealing between two persons involving 'money' or a dealing, which can be expressed in terms of money.

By now it should be clear that we are talking of recording and accounting terms of 'money' or currency. In India, we record all transactions in rupees; in U.S.A. it is recorded in U.S.dollars, and so on.

We should bear in mind that in a business all transactions are recorded only in one currency. Where there are transactions involving foreign currency (like in transactions of import/export), the foreign currencies have to be converted to Indian rupees at approximate exchange rates and then recorded.

entry

What is an entry? The expression 'entry' must have been evolved from the word 'to enter'. Entry really signifies the actual process of recording the transaction or 'writing' the transaction in the book of business.

Account

This is another term which must be clearly understood before we go ahead, though most of the readers must have heard and come across this terminology, very often. An account is basically a name or a title under which transactions of the same nature are recorded. For example, we can have 'Cash Account' where only transactions of cash will be recorded.

In general, 'to account' would mean 'to record'. The word account is used in relation to both specific names or in relation to groups of transactions. For example, we can say Mr. A's account or we could say personal accounts. The word account is normally written as A/C for short. This, I believe is only for convenience and not because accountants believe in shortcuts!

Types of Accounts

The various transactions in a business have been grouped into three types of accounts:

Real Accounts: These accounts are for transactions pertaining to tangibles like cash, machinery, materials and so on. A bank account (though conceptually not tangible to us) is also grouped here because it really represents cash.

Personal Accounts: These accounts are for transactions relating to persons. E.g. Mr.A's account or Mr.X's accounts and so on.

Nominal Accounts: These are accounts for transactions of Income and Expense. E.g. wages, repairs or sales. Also, we can say all transactions, which are neither 'real accounts' nor 'personal accounts' are 'nominal accounts'.

The Debit and The Credit

We have earlier talked of the dual aspect or the double-entry for every transaction. For identifying these two aspects of the transaction they have to be named. One aspect is called "debit" and the other aspect is called "credit". In reality, debit and credit are only names and do not have any other intrinsic meaning as such.

We can, therefore, now say that for every transaction there will be some account, which will be debited, and some account will be credited.

For every debit there must be a corresponding credit, and both the debit and the credit must be for the same amount.

From this it must follow that when any account is debited with an amount, there will always have to be another corresponding account, which will be credited by the same amount. In reality, however, the number of accounts to be debited or credited could be more than one at a time, but even in such cases the total amount of the debits will be equal to the total amount of the credits.

The Accounting Process

I am yet to meet a person who has not heard of a voucher or a ledger. These are essential implements in the accounting process. Let us get to know these a little more.

The Original Accounting Record: Voucher

An accounting record in any business organization will originate on a piece of paper (normally standardized and properly formatted) which is called a 'Voucher'. A voucher, of course is the general name – the more specific names would be for example, cash voucher for purchase transaction, bank voucher for bank transaction, journal voucher and so on.

There is nothing very sacrosanct about these names and there could be a slight variation in their nomenclature in different organizations.

A voucher contains the complete details about a particular transaction that takes place. It also contains the amount of the transaction. The transaction is recorded into the account books from the vouchers. Since vouchers are the primary records of a transaction, it is very important that they are prepared and retained properly, as neatly as possible!

The Books of Accounts

The vouchers have to be entered, or an 'entry' has to be made in the bills of accounts.

The recording of transaction is done in two stages.

First stage: Here all transactions have to be first written down in the account books in a chronological sequence. This has to be done very accurately indicating the debits and credits properly, and after ensuring that all transactions are entered. It is one of the most important functions of an accountant to ensure that all transactions have been recorded in the books. For our understanding, we will call the accounts books used in this first stage as primary books of accounts. Some of the common names of primary books are Cash Book, Bank Book, Purchase and Sales Registers and so on.

Second stage: From the primary books of accounts, we then move on to the secondary books of accounts. These are known as ledgers. In ledgers, classified records of transactions are maintained accounts-head-wise.

We have seen that in the primary books all entries are only entered chronologically. How then, will we know, for example, the totals of transactions under the various account heads?

Suppose that, we have to find out the total expenses in the year towards wages or repairs, or if we want to know the total value of machinery purchased to data. Such informations cannot be easily collected from the primary books and marked out the relevant transactions before taking a total of all such transactions. This process would not only be cumbersome but in actual practice, be an unrealistic way of working.

What is therefore done in the ledger is that different accounts heads are 'opened' on different pages or leaves (known in accounting terminology as 'folios') and the transactions from the primary books are 'posted' or written under the relevant account heads on the appropriate debit or credit side. When the process of posting is complete we would automatically have all the transactions transferred into the ledgers properly classified or categorized under the different account heads and also bifurcated as debits and credits.

Trial Balance

It would be clear that if the 'balance' from all the ledger accounts are listed down accurately, showing in each case whether the balance is a debit or credit and then a total of the debit and credit balances are taken, the two balances would be equal (or would 'tally').

The final act in the process of accounting involves the preparation of such a statement. This statement is called the 'Trial Balance'. Many people use an expression 'Trial Balance Sheet'. Actually there is nothing like this in accounting. It is a misconception. The trial balance will contain the 'net balance' or summaries of all accounts as on a particular date (covering transactions for the period up to that date).

Once the trial balance is properly prepared with the debit and credit totals tallied, the basic activity of recording transactions can be said to be completed. In actual practice, especially in organizations where accounting is done in the manual process, this exercise of tallying the trail balance becomes a big nightmare and people in the accounts department actually entertain themselves with a 'party' or a 'treat' to celebrate the tallying of the trial, balance. Sadly, with the advent of computerization in the field of financial accounting, this thrill of tallying the trail balance is slowly becoming a thing of the past.

The outputs of the accounting process are the Profit and Loss Account and Balance Sheet.

Some More Concepts

After going through the mechanics of accounting, and before we look at the Profit and Loss Account and Balance Sheet, it will be worthwhile knowing and understanding some of the important terminologies that are very frequently used in the finance and accounting fields.

Assets

Assets of a business are what the business owns — some of the assets may be tangible in nature, like cash, machinery, furniture or stocks. Some assets could be intangible like 'amounts to be collected' or Debtor's Balance, where these amounts are 'due' to the business by outsiders.

Liabilities

Liabilities of a business are what the business owes. Some of the examples would be 'Loans from banks' or 'Creditors'. These amounts are 'due to' outsiders by the business.

Expenses

Expenses are amount spent by the business for the purpose of 'running' the business and for actual use in production of 'goods and services', which are to be sold. Examples would be raw material, wages, repairs etc.

Incomes

Incomes are amounts earned by the business. The major source of incomes will naturally be the sale of goods and services. There are also other smaller types of income that a business earns, like interest, rent, etc.

Inflow And Outflows

When cash or funds come into the business they are referred to as 'inflow' and when cash as funds go out of the business they are referred to as 'outflows'.

An inflow of cash or funds will either: (i) mean an income or, (ii) create a liability.

Outflow of cash or funds will either (i) mean an expense or, (ii) generate an asset.

Capital And Revenue Expenses

The general understanding is that whenever the business spends something it incurs an expense. There is a slight differentiation to be made here.

Any spending could be on either of two accounts: i) To acquire an asset or, ii) To incur an expense.

To distinguish between these two types of spending they are called Capital Expenditure and Revenue Expense.

A Capital Expenditure results into an asset whereas a Revenue Expense results into expense. Revenue Expenses are expenses incurred for purchase of goods and services, which are required for immediate use and also for carrying on the day-to-day activities of the business. Revenue Expenses are for a particular year or period and are always incurred to earn incomes in that year or period. Revenue Expenses are reduced from incomes to arrive at profits.

Capital Expenditure on the other hand is incurred for items which have a long life and are therefore used over a period of time. Capital Expenditure results in creation of an asset, which has a long enduring benefit to the business. For example, machinery is a capital expenditure, it has a long life and is used for a long period. This is an asset of the business— something that the business owns and uses for its activities. We can also call capital expenditure as expenditure for the company's infrastructure.

Normally, amounts spent for items of revenue nature are referred to as 'expenses' and amount spent for items of capital nature are called 'expenditure'.

The concept of inflow and outflow will be clear from the flowchart in Table B.

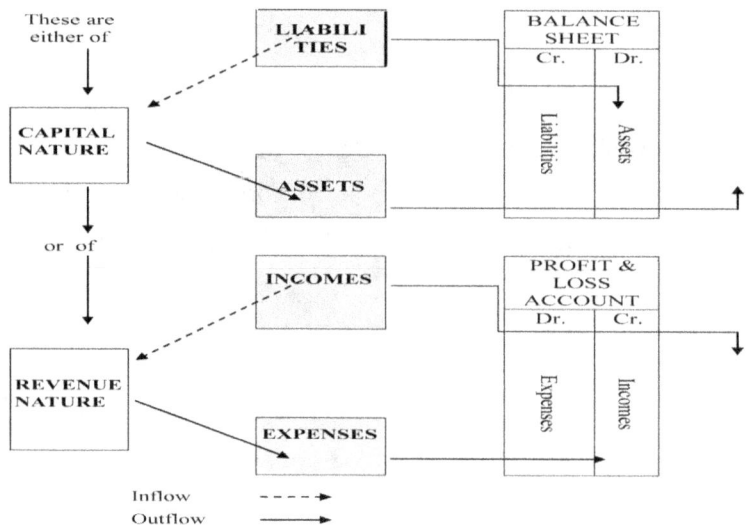

Accounting Year

The accounting year is the calendar chosen for itself by the business. It is the period for which the performance of the business is worked out. The accounting year in normal cases is a one-year period but it could be any period of one year not necessarily the period from January to December. This period is chosen by the business on various considerations. The most commonly used accounting years are those starting on January or April or July or October, but there is no hard and fast rule for this. Traditional Indian businesses have their accounting year from April to March. Many foreign companies have accounting years on a '52 week ending' basis. This concept has undergone some change in view of the uniform accounting year introduced recently in the Direct Tax Laws. It is expected that most of the businesses would switch over to the accounting year April to March.

Performance of companies are prepared and published in relation to the accounting year, though for internal purposes, these reports are prepared even on monthly/quarterly basis.

The final Accounts

Now that we are sufficiently armed with the basic accounting jargons, let us venture to look at the Balance Sheet and Profit and Loss Accounts.

Balance Sheet (B/S)

The Balance Sheet is a statement of the company's assets and liabilities on a particular date. It gives the status 'at a point of time' and not 'for a period'. The Balance Sheet has to be prepared as on the closing date of the company's accounting year.

It contains details of the various assets owned by the company and the various liabilities owned by the company. Double entry principles require that the total assets and total liabilities of business have to 'tally' or 'balance', i.e. Total Assets equal to Total Liabilities.

The balancing of Total Assets and Liabilities in a Balance Sheet, apart from ensuring the proper implementation of the Double Entry System, confirms the concept of business being a 'separate entity'. A business can create assets only out of the liabilities that it has taken on, and therefore these two have to necessarily match. Though it sounds strange the first liability of any business is the owner or the shareholders, because as soon as the owner brings in the capital, the business (which is a separate legal entity) becomes indebted to the owner to the extent of the capital that has been brought in. In other words, the capital is the liability of the business to the owner or shareholders (in case of companies).

The basic information to be disclosed and the manner of the presentation of this information are statutorily prescribed (for Private and Public Companies) by the Indian Companies Act, 1956. The Act lays down the minimum levels of disclosure; the Company however is free to disclose more.

All individual accounts head will not appear in the Balance Sheet as such, but they will be suitably summarized and consolidated under broad categories. For example, the Balance Sheet will not give a list of all the debtors of the company but only the total amount of all the debtors. Similarly, it will not list down the individual items of inventory (or stocks) but only the total value of the inventory.

Profit And Loss Account (P & L A/c.)

The Profit and Loss Account (P & L A/c.) is a statement prepared at the end of the accounting year to show the details of the incomes and expenses of the year. To be clear, this statement, unlike the balance sheet, is prepared 'for a period'. A profit and loss account can also be prepared for shorter periods, say monthly or quarterly.

In this statement various expenses accounts, duly summarized and consolidated, are listed on one side (i.e. the debit side) and the various incomes are listed on the other side (i.e. the credit side). If the income side total (i.e. the credit side) is more than the expense side total (i.e. the debit side) the profit and loss account will indicate a profit for the year or vice versa.

There are also statutory disclosure rules which are applicable for the profit and loss account under the Indian Companies Act, 1956.

Both, the annual profit and loss account and the balance sheet, are required to be signed by the Directors, the Company Secretary, and audited by the Statutory Auditors of the Company.

The profit and loss accounts and the balance sheet are also referred to as the final accounts.

Balance Sheet Terminologies

Before we go ahead, let us look at some of the major items that appear in the Balance Sheet, more closely. This would give us a clear understanding of what they mean. We will start with the assets side:

Fixed Assets

Fixed Assets of the company having a very long life span. They are brought into the business with the idea that they will remain for very long in the business, and therefore, they are called Fixed Assets. They are:

1) Plant and Machinery
2) Electrical Installations
3) Office Equipment
4) Vehicles
5) Furniture / Fixtures
6) Land
7) Building etc.

These assets do not move in and out of the business regularly but remain in the business in the same form and constitute the basic infrastructure of the business activity.

Current Assets

Current Assets consist of assets which keep moving in and out of business. These assets change their form very frequently, e.g. when a 'Debtor' pays up, it gets converted into the form of 'Cash', these assets are required for the actual working of the business on a day-to-day basis.

Current Assets are also called 'Liquid Assets' because they are in a form in which they can be converted to cash, within a short period. Cash is the most liquid asset. In today's situation liquidity in a company is of paramount importance.

The entire group of Current Assets is also known as Gross Working Capital. Working Capital means capital or assets required for the day-to-day working of the business. Working Capital control is a very important area of management control and action; we will be discussing this aspect in greater detail at a later stage.

On the Liabilities side, we have:

Share Capital

This is the amount of owner's funds that have been put into the business. In case of Companies, the capital is brought in by giving 'shares' to the investors. The Share Capital is the liability with the longest life span. In fact share capital will remain as long as the business remains.

Reserves

Reserves are 'accumulated profit earned and retained in the business over the years'. The process by which reserves are created is known as appropriation from profit. There are some reserves which need to be made statutorily; the other reserves are discretionary reserves. Reserves belong to the shareholders; and are therefore generally grouped under 'Shareholder's funds'. The other common expression used for creating reserves is 'ploughing back of profits'.

The word appropriation in a way means 'keeping aside'. When the company arrives at the final figure of profit after tax, it has to decide how these profits are to be used. The normal requirements are:

i) For paying dividends to shareholders,

ii) For creating statutory reserves,

iii) For reuse or recirculation in the business.

Secured Loans

These are the loans borrowed by the company. These loans are usually taken from the banks, financial institutions and from the money market by issuing debentures. These loans are called 'secured' because for the lenders there is a firm security of repayment. This security is given by 'hypothecating' or 'mortgaging' specified assets of the company, to the lenders, for these loans. These loans normally have a long repayment period.

Cash Credit or overdraft from banks are also grouped as secured Loans, because these are also secured (the security is usually the stocks and Debtors). We could call these as Working Capital Loans. Legally speaking, the bank facilities, like overdraft and cash credit are of short term duration, but in practice, especially, on account of the perpetuity of business, these ultimately turn out to be permanent loans to the company.

These loans have fixed interest rates. Usually on long term loans which are taken for acquiring fixed assets, the rates of interest would vary between 10–14%. Debentures carry a rate varying between 13.5%–14.5%. The bank cash credit / overdraft interest rate at present is 17.5% p.a. These interest rates are governed by the Reserve Bank of India (RBI) and could keep changing, depending upon the R.B.I. policies and guidelines.

Unsecured Loans

These are loans taken by the company, but these are 'clean' loans. The only security for these loans is the company's image and credibility. Fixed Deposits which are raised from public are also unsecured loans.

Current Liabilities / Loans Advances

This group includes short term loans and other liabilities. The major item in this group is the Sundry Creditors, i.e. amount due to be paid to suppliers for goods and services purchased from them on credit. Loans and advances here refer mainly to deposits or advances received from customers against their orders on the company.

> *Provisions*
>
> We often come across this item on the Liabilities side of the Balance Sheet. The items that are most commonly seen are Provision for Taxation and Provision for Dividends.
>
> The provision refers to a future liability which is required to be met out of profits of the company. By making a provision or by providing, the company actually keeps aside this amount before any other appropriation is made from the profits.
>
> The word 'provision', is also very commonly used in another context. At the end of the year when the company's accounts are finalized the accountant has to ensure that all expenses which the company has incurred are actually reflected in the books. At the year end, for a variety of reasons, all accounting documents may not be fully ready to be put through the accounting system. The accountant makes an exhaustive list and accounts these expenses in the books of accounts. Such entries are made by journal entries. This procedure of accounting for unbooked expenses is commonly known as making 'provisions for expenses'.

Two Systems Of Maintaining Accounts

This discussion on provisions for expenses leads us to the next topic. There are two accepted systems of accounting

a) Mercantile System

b) Cash System

Mercantile System of accounting requires that a business accounts for all its expenses that have been incurred to earn its income. To put it simply, if one has earned certain incomes for which certain expenses have been incurred, one must ensure that all the expenses that have been incurred whether paid for or not, whether the paperwork is complete or not, are accounted as expenses. The mercantile system is followed by all the businesses which are engaged in manufacturing, trading or such similar activities. The amendments in the Companies Act have now made it compulsory for all companies to follow mercantile system of accounting.

Cash System of accounting records only such expenses which have actually been paid for. Similarly the cash system records only such income which has actually come in cash. The cash system is commonly followed by professionals like doctor, advocates, architects, chartered accountants and others.

The other point that one must note in this context, is that whichever system, i.e. mercantile or cash, is followed, one must follow it consistently every year and not keep changing it from year to year. Consistency in accounting practices is a very important requirement for a good system of accounting.

Depreciation — A Charge For Use Of Fixed Assets

We have seen earlier that any outflow would either result in an expense or in the creation of assets. We have also noted that revenue expenses are taken to the profit and loss account to be charged off against incomes.

Now let us explore a peculiar phenomenon by which some assets get converted into expenses. We will see two of the most common type of assets which undergo such a change.

Current Assets

Under current assets, we have group inventory items, like raw materials, stores and spares and work-in-progress. As long as these are in stock and not used, these are assets of the business but as soon as these are used for manufacturing or 'consumed', these become expenses.

Fixed Assets

The fixed assets of a company have a very long life span, but the fact remains that at some stage, by natural process of wear and tear, or also on account of obsolescence, the effective value of these assets may become negligible or in many cases even zero. When this happens what will happen to the figures of fixed assets in the Balance Sheet?

Let us look at this problem from another angle also. In our profit and loss Account, we account for all costs of the business, but we do not recognize any cost towards the use of fixed assets. This does not seem very logical, does it?

To take care of this problem, we have the concept of depreciation.

Depreciation

Depreciation is an annual charge made in the profit and loss account to recognize that the fixed assets undergo wear and tear on account of their use. Every year in the accounts, an amount (called depreciation) is accounted as an expense for the year and the amount is kept aside in a reserve called the 'Depreciation Reserve'. This reserve keeps growing each year and is expected to help the business to prepare for the eventual scrapping of the old asset and replacement of those assets by new acquisition.

In the balance sheet, the original cost of the fixed assets is reduced by the amount of the depreciation reserve, and only the net amount is reflected. This ensures that only the depreciated value of the assets, after considering the wear and tear and diminution in the life of the assets, is reflected in the balance sheet. When we go on charging depreciation on fixed assets year after year, it automatically means that over a period of time, the fixed assets are also converted into expenses.

Depreciation is a statutory resure charged in the profit and loss account. Profits of a company cannot be correctly determined unless depreciation is considered. Depreciation is the only 'non-cash' expenses which are considered in the profit and loss account. No depreciation is calculated for 'land'.

There are two commonly used methods of calculating depreciation:

Written Down Value Method: (WDV)

Example: Let's say oiriginal cost is	Rs.100
Ist Year depreciation @ 30%	Rs.30
WDV at the end of the first year.	Rs.70
2nd Year Depreciation @ 30% on WDV	Rs.70

The depreciation rates to be used for the different categories of assets are laid down in the Income Tax Act and also in the Companies Act.

We understand from the above example that the amount of depreciation for an asset will keep reducing every year, since the written down value also gets reduced with the annual charges.

Straight Line Method: (SLM)

In this method, the amount of depreciation will remain constant each year and the method is therefore called straight line method. The rates for straight line depreciation are worked out in relation to the expected life of the asset. The amount of depreciation under SLM every year remains constant because the rate is applied to the original cost instead of the WDV. Obviously the corresponding straight-line rate is lower than the WDV rate.

At present the rates of depreciation under the Income Tax Act and the Companies Act have been delinked. Under the Income Tax Act, only written down value method of charging depreciation is recognized and for the purpose of applying rates all assets have been classified under blocks of assets as follows:

Rates of Depreciation (General Rates)

Buildings	5%
Plant & Machinery	33.33%
Furnitures	10%
Ships	20%

Under the Companies Act, 1956, after the passing of the recent amendments, the rates specified are as follows.

Rate	SL Rate	WDV
	%	%
1) Factory Buildings	3.34	10
2) Plant & Machinery (General Rate)	5.15*	15*
3) Motor Cars, Scooters, other two wheelers	7.07	20
4) Trucks, Buses	11.31	30
5) Furniture & Fittings	3.34	10

*Extra shifts allowance is to be provided if factory runs for mare than one shift as under:-

	SL	WDV
1 Shift	5.15	15
2 Shifts	8.09	22.5
3 Shifts	11.31	30

The Companies Act also expects the method and 'rates' used for providing depreciation to be mentioned in the accounts.

Apart from knowing the rates and methodology, it is important that we understand the concept of depreciation. There are some who do not consider depreciation as an expense since they do not see it being actually incurred. These persons wake up only when they find at some stage later that their fixed asset has become useless or unusable. The value at that time will truly be zero and will therefore require that the balance sheet reflects such assets at zero value by writing off the amount, through the profit and loss account. This situation could prove disastrous for the business.

There is also no hard and fast rule about the rates. The rates prescribed under the Income Tax Act are more in the nature of incentives to the industries and business. The SL and the WDV rates in the Companies Act are based in a general assessment of the expected 'useful life of the assets'. However, a business may, in appropriate cases, consider the prescribed rates to be too low or too high and modify the rates accordingly for his own business.

Depreciation, it should be remembered, not only provides for wear and tear but also for obsolescence.

Chapter 7

Different Types of Taxes in India

"When there is an income tax, the just man will pay more and the unjust less on the same amount of income."

Plato, The Republic (427 BC–347 BC)
Greek author & philosopher in Athens

A brieF oVerVieW oF the tAX structure in inDiA

Tax is the amount paid by the citizens of a country to their rulers or government for providing defence, policing, judiciary, welfare and other administrative support. Governments derive their right to tax the subject from the Constitution. The Constitution of India has distributed the power to make laws between the Central Government and the State Government. Thus taxation in India is both a Central Government subject as well as a State Government subject.

Direct tax Vs. indirect tax

Direct tax is one where the tax is paid by the person who will ultimately bear the burden. The best example is Income Tax.

In the case of an Indirect Tax, there is a disconnect between the actual collection of the levy and its burden. For example, a trader who sells goods, collects Value Added Tax (VAT) and remits it to the government but the burden is actually borne by the customer who has to finally pay for it.

Given below are some of the well known taxes in India:

(a) *Income Tax*: This is a direct tax and is governed by the Income Tax Act, 1961. Under the act there are five heads of income namely Salary, Rental income, Capital Gains, Business Income and Income from other sources. There is a proposal to change the existing direct taxes with a framework popularly known as Direct Tax Code.

(b) *Wealth Tax*: Indians are also subject to Wealth Tax in respect of specified assets like vacant urban land, jewellery, motor cars, yachts, bullion and cash. The rate of wealth tax is 1% on wealth exceeding Rs.30 lakhs.

(c) *Excise Duty*: The taxable event which occasions the imposition of the levy is manufacture of goods. Excise duty is payable at the time when goods are cleared from the factory or place of manufacture irrespective of actual sales.

(d) *Service Tax*: This has been replaced by GST

(e) *Customs duty*: When goods are imported into India, customs duty is payable on the landed cost of the goods.

Chapter 8

Costing

"He that is of the opinion money will do everything may well be suspected of doing everything for money. "

Benjamin Franklin (1706–1790)
US author, diplomat, inventor, physicist, politician & printer

cost controL AnD reDuction

the nature of cost

Cost may be defined as –

(i) The amount of expenditure (actual or notional) incurred on or attributable to a given product, job, activity, or cost object.

(ii) Cost represents the resources that have been or must be sacrificed to attain a particular objective. Sacrifice may be direct or indirect.

A **cost object** is any product or activity for which a separate measurement of costs is desired. In other words, if the users of accounting information want to know the cost of something, this something is called a cost object. Examples of cost objects include the cost of a product, the cost of rendering a service to a bank customer or hospital patient, the cost of operating a particular department or sales territory, or indeed anything for which one wants to measure the cost of resources used.

Costing is the process of determining the cost of doing something, e.g., the cost of manufacturing an article, rendering a service or performing a function. The article manufactured, service rendered or function performed is known as the objects of costing. Objects of costing are always activities.

The cost collection system typically accounts for costs in two broad stages;

1. It accumulates costs by classifying them into certain categories such as labour, materials and overhead costs (or by cost behaviour such as fixed and variable).

2. It then traces these costs to cost objects.

Cost accounting is concerned with the calculation of product costs for use in the financial accounts while **Management accounting** serves managers by providing information to help them in decision-making, planning and control. Cost Accounting information is required for a variety of reasons, and it is essential that a sound system of recording and classifying this information be established.

cost classification

The clear understanding of various cost concepts is essential for a study of cost control and cost reduction.

Cost object categories	Possible methods of cost classification
1. Cost for stock valuation	Period and product costs. Elements of manufacturing costs
2. Costs for decision-making	Relevant and irrelevant costs
	Avoidable and unavoidable costs
	Sunk costs
	Opportunity costs
	Marginal and incremental costs
3. Costs for control	Controllable and uncontrollable costs

Costs Based for Stock Valuation

Period and product costs

Product cost is the aggregate of costs that are associated with a unit of a product. Such costs may or may not include an element of overheads depending upon the type of costing system in force—absorption or direct. Product costs are related to goods produced or purchased for resale and are initially identifiable as part of inventory. These product or inventory costs become expenses in the form of cost of goods sold only when the inventory is sold. Product cost is associated with unit of output. The costs of inputs in forming the product viz., the direct material, direct labour and factory overhead constitute the product costs.

The product cost is a cost that tends to be unaffected by changes in level of activity during a given period of time. Period cost is associated with a time period rather than manufacturing activity and these costs are deducted as expenses during the current period without being classified as product costs. Selling and distribution costs are period costs and are deducted from the revenue without their being regarded as part of the inventory cost.

Element-wise classification of costs

The elements of cost can be studied as direct and indirect costs. If the object of interest for identifying and measuring cost is to determine how much sacrifice is involved in manufacturing a particular product, then initially one can define the three elements of total cost as (a) Materials, (b) Labour and (c) Expenses.

All these costs may be direct or indirect costs.

Direct costs (traceable costs): Direct costs are those which can be identified easily and indisputably with a unit of operation or costing unit or cost centre. Costs of direct material, direct labour and direct expenses can be directly allocated or identified with particular cost centres or cost units and can be directly charged to such cost centres or cost units. These costs are also called traceable costs.

Indirect costs (common costs): Indirect costs cannot be allocated but can be apportioned to cost centres or cost units. These costs are also called common costs. The indirect costs are not traceable to any plant, department, and operation or to any individual final product. All overhead costs are indirect costs. Cost of indirect material, indirect labour and indirect expenses in aggregate constitute the overhead costs and are the indirect component of the total costs. Indirect costs that cannot be directly allocated to cost units or cost centres and have to be absorbed or recovered in cost units are termed as indirect costs. The concepts of direct and indirect costs are meaningless without identification of the relevant cost unit or cost centre. Segregation of costs into direct and indirect costs is essential for proper accounting and control of costs and also for managerial decision-making purpose.

Advanced manufacturing technologies such as Robotics, Computer Aided Design and Manufacture, Flexible Manufacturing Systems, Optimized Production, Technology, Just-in-Time etc., are revolutionizing the design of manufacturing at shop-floor, quality etc., creating areas for improved opportunities. They have dramatically changed the manufacturing cost behavior patterns. The direct cost component of product cost is decreasing while depreciation, engineering and information processing costs are increasing. These changes have resulted in higher overhead rates and a shrinking base of direct cost over which to allocate those costs.

Cost for Decision-Making

Relevant and Irrelevant costs: The relevant cost is a cost appropriate in aiding to make specific management decisions. Business decisions involve planning for future and consideration of several alternative courses of action. In this process the costs which are affected by the decisions are future costs. Such costs are called relevant costs because they are pertinent to the decisions in hand, the cost is said to be relevant if it helps the manager in taking a right decision in furtherance of the company's objectives.

For example, where a company intends to rearrange production facilities, the estimates of future costs are as under:

Item of cost	Existing facilities	Proposed re-arrangement
Direct material/unit	25.00	25.00
Direct Labour/unit	15.00	10.00

The material cost being constant, it is irrelevant to the decision. The relevant cost is labour cost.

Escapable or avoidable and unavoidable cost: The escapable cost is an avoidable cost that will not be incurred if an activity is not undertaken or discontinued. Avoidable cost will often correspond with variable costs. Avoidable cost can be identified with an activity or sector of a business and which would be avoided if that activity or sector did not exist. The escapable costs refer to costs which can be reduced due to a contraction in the activities of a business enterprise. It is the net effect on costs that is important, not just the costs directly avoidable by the contraction.

Examples

> - Closing an apparently unprofitable branch house-storage, cost of other branches and transportation charges would increase.
> - Reducing credit sales - costs estimated may be less than the benefits otherwise available.

Escapable costs are different from controllable and discretionary costs.

The **sunk costs** are those costs that have been invested in a project and which will not be recovered if the project is terminated. The sunk cost is one for which the expenditure has taken place in the past. This cost is not affected by a particular decision under consideration. Sunk costs are always the results of decisions in future. Investment in plant and machinery, as soon as it is installed, is sunk cost and is not relevant for decision. Amortisation of past expenses e.g., depreciation is sunk cost. Sunk cost will remain the same irrespective of the alternative selected. Thus, it need not be considered by the management in evaluating the alternatives as it is common to all of them.

The **opportunity cost** is the value of a benefit sacrificed in favour of an alternative course of action. It is the maximum amount that could be obtained at any given point of time if a resource was sold or put to the most valuable alternative use that would be practicable. The opportunity cost of a good or service is measured in terms of revenue which could have been earned by employing that good or service in other alternative uses. Opportunity cost can be defined as the revenue forgone by not making the best alternative use. Opportunity cost is the prospective change in cost following the adoption of an alternative machine process, raw materials etc. It is the cost of opportunity lost by diversion of an input factor from one use to another.

The **marginal cost** is the variable cost of one unit of a product or a service i.e., a cost which would be avoided if the unit was not produced or provided. In this context a unit is usually either a single article or a standard measure such as litre or kilogram, but may, in certain circumstances, be an operation, process or part of an organisation. The marginal cost is the amount at any given volume of output by which aggregate costs are changed if the volume of output is increased or decreased by one unit. The marginal costing technique is the process of ascertaining marginal costs and of the effects of changes in volume or type of output on profit by differentiating between fixed and variable costs.

The **incremental cost** is the extra cost of taking one course of action rather than another. It is hence also called differential cost. The incremental cost is the additional cost due to a change in the level or nature of business activity. The change may take several forms changing the channel of distribution, adding a new machine, replacing a machine by a better machine, execution of export order etc. Incremental costs will be different in case of different alternatives. Hence, incremental costs are relevant to the management in the analysis for decision-making.

classification for exercising control over costs

The costs can be classified into Engineered, Managed and Capacity costs for exercising control over costs. This classification is based on the following factors:

- The accuracy with which the relationship between the inputs to and outputs from a process can be determined, and
- The time span between the introduction of the input and the completion of the output, i.e., the production cycle or process time.

Engineered cost

The engineered costs relate to the inputs like material, labour and expenses, etc., which are directly connected with the product. The quality or material usage or labour hours can be determined for each product or activity. An item of engineered cost is a type of input that has a definite physical relationship with output. In most of the production processes it is possible to develop standards for both direct materials and direct labour and these standards reflect the relationship between input and output. Engineered costs can be established with the help of (1) engineering analysis and (2) analysis of historical costs and can be controlled by the management by scheduling production volume, taking proper care of machinery and assigning workers to various jobs.

Managed cost

The managed cost is a cost that stems from current operations but which must continue to be incurred into the future, its same level determined by management, to ensure the continued existence of the enterprise. The managed costs are those which have no direct relationship with the product. The cost on advertisement, research and development, tool room, drawings and design, etc., cannot be easily associated with the product. The control system starts with annual budgets for these costs. Comparison of actual costs with budget is made on a monthly basis and variations are ascertained. Managed costs produce an output which benefit the firm relationship between the amount of managed costs incurred (input) and its output.

Capacity cost

The capacity costs are normally fixed costs. A definite relationship between capacity costs and the output of product emerge only in the long-run. The cost distribution by a company for providing production, administration and selling and distribution capabilities in order to enable it to perform its functions are termed as capacity costs. Capacity costs are in the nature of long-term costs and are incurred as a result of planning decisions. The input and output relationship for the above three types of costs are shown below:

Item of cost	Input-output relationship	Time lag between Input and Output
Engineered cost	Strong	Short
Managed costs	Weak	Moderate
Capacity costs	Strong	Long

Fixed cost vs variable cost

Variable cost

The variable cost is a cost that tends to vary in accordance with the level of activity within the relevant range and within a given period of time. The prime product costs i.e., direct material, direct labour and direct expenses tend to vary in direct proportion to the level of activity. An increase in the volume means a proportionate increase in the total variable costs and a decrease in volume will lead to a proportionate decline in the total variable costs. There is a linear relationship between volume and variable costs. They are constant per unit.

Fixed cost

The fixed cost is a cost that tends to be unaffected by changes in the level of activity during a given period of time. The fixed costs remain constant in total, regardless of changes in volume upto a certain level of output. They are not affected by changes in the volume of production. There is an inverse relationship between volume and fixed cost per unit. Fixed costs tend to remain constant for all levels of activity within a certain range. It follows that some fixed costs will continue to be incurred even when the activity comes down to nil. Some fixed costs are liable to change from one period to another; for example, salaries bill may go up because of annual increments or due to change in the pay structure. From control point of view fixed costs are analysed into the following:

Committed Cost

These are the committed costs that are primarily associated with maintaining the company's legal and physical existence over which management has little discretion, e.g., insurance premiums, rates and taxes, rent etc. Some committed costs have to be incurred even if there is a shutdown.

Managed Cost

The managed cost is a cost that stems from current operations but which must continue to be incurred into the future, at the same level determined by the management, to ensure the continued existence of the enterprise. For e.g., management and staff salaries are related to current operations but which must continue to be paid to ensure the continued operating existence of the company.

Programmed Cost

The programmed cost is a cost that is subject to both the management discretion and management control but which has little immediate relevance to current operations although it is generally incurred to ensure long-term survival. Programmed costs are subject both to management discretion and management control, but which are unrelated to current activities and it appears that these costs result from special policy decisions of management.

Being in the nature of policy costs, fixed costs are by and large controllable by the top management and not controllable at the shop floor. From decision- making point of view, whether a cost is fixed or variable will depend upon the decision under consideration and this will determine the appropriate time span and hence the nature of the cost.

Chapter 9

Return on Investment

"A banker is a fellow who lends you his umbrella when the sun is shining, but wants it back the minute it begins to rain."

Mark Twain (1835–1910)
US humorist, novelist, short story author & wit

FinAnciAL rAtio AnALysis

The Balance Sheet records the assets and liabilities of a company as on a date. This is usually the 31st of March in India, though, this need not always be the case. It is more appropriate to view the Balance Sheet as a statement that shows where the company's money is invested and how these investments have been funded. In this sense the assets are termed **Application of Funds** and the liabilities are termed **Sources of Funds**. The Balance Sheet is supported by the Profit & Loss Account which explains the revenues generated by the firm and gives an accurate picture of the profit earned for the period. These are complementary documents that provide a clear picture of the company's financial strengths and weaknesses.

But, a direct scrutiny or comparison of these documents on a stand alone basis might not be very fruitful as absolute figures are sometimes meaningless.

> For example, to know that a company made a profit of Rs.84 crores is interesting but not useful. We really do not know whether Rs.84 crores is good or bad. For this we would have to compare the profit with the net sales. This would give us a percentage which can now be compared with a similar percentage of the previous comparable period. This is called **Intra Firm Comparison**. It may also be compared with the similar percentage of a competitor. This is called **Inter Firm Comparison**. The process of converting the figures in the Balance Sheet into such comparable indicators is popularly known as **Financial Ratio Analysis.**

Let us now proceed to analyze the financial statements and thereby obtain a better understanding of the business model and profits of the company.

Ratios can be categorized into five types as follows:
1. Profitability Ratios
2. Performance Ratios
3. Liquidity Ratios

4. Solvency Ratios
5. Market Test Ratios

Profitability ratios

1. Operating Margin Ratio (OMR)

$$\text{Operating Margin Ratio} = \frac{\text{Operating Margin}}{\text{Net Sales}} \times 100$$

This ratio enables direct comparison of the operating capabilities irrespective of the ability of the company to source funds at low interest and plan for taxes and its income from non-core business. Operating Margin is also known as Contribution. Where a company has more than one business this ratio may be calculated for each business.

2. EBDITA Ratio (Earnings Before Depreciation Interest Tax & Amortization)

$$\text{EBDITA} = \frac{\text{EBDITA}}{\text{Net Sales}} \times 100$$

EBDITA is considered an important indicator of profitability as it reveals the ability of a business to generate profits better than its competitors in a given industry. Depreciation is a non-cash notional estimate and is therefore not considered. Interest is a function of the company's leveraging i.e. quantum of debt used to fund the assets and taxes are dependent on managerial policy and financial wizardry. So if you are just interested in knowing whether a company is profitable as a business, this ratio is quite useful.

3. Profit After Tax Ratio (PAT)

$$\text{Profit After Tax Ratio} = \frac{\text{PAT}}{\text{Sales}} \times 100$$

The ultimate profitability ratio PAT is also known as the Bottom-line. If this ratio is lower than the industry average, the company is in serious trouble.

4. Expense Ratio

$$\text{Expense Ratio} = \frac{\text{Raw Material}}{\text{Sales}} \times 100$$

Performance ratios

Operating cycle is the key to profitability. In other words, the number of times we can Turnover the assets. Therefore these ratios are also called Turnover Ratios. These ratios are given as number of times.

i) Fixed Assets Turnover Ratio $= \dfrac{\text{Net Sales}}{\text{Average Fixed Assets}}$

ii) Working Capital Turnover Ratio $= \dfrac{\text{Net Sales}}{\text{Average Working Capital}}$

iii) Inventory Turnover Ratio $= \dfrac{\text{Net Sales}}{\text{Average Inventory}}$

Conversion Cycle (Days) $= \dfrac{365}{\text{Inventory Turnover}}$

iv) Debtor Turnover Ratio $= \dfrac{\text{Net Sales}}{\text{Average Debtors}}$

v) Debtor Collection Cycle $= \dfrac{365}{\text{Debtors Turnover}}$

vi) Creditors Payment $= \dfrac{\text{Average Creditors}}{\text{Purchases}} \times 365$

vii) Equity Turnover Ratio $= \dfrac{\text{Net Sales}}{\text{Share Holders Funds}}$

Return On Investment

This is a powerful indicator of performance and profitability. This ratio is a numerical articulation of Peter F. Drucker's famous quote "It is not enough if you do things right you should do the right things". Doing things Right is indicated by high performance ratios. Doing the right things is validated by a high profitability percentage. The combination of the two is a high Return On Investment (ROI).

$$\text{Return on Investment} = \dfrac{\text{Sales}}{\text{Shareholders Funds}} \times \dfrac{\text{PAT}}{\text{Sales}} = \dfrac{\text{PAT}}{\text{Shareholders Funds}}$$

Shareholders Funds

= (Share Capital + Reserves & Surplus) − (Miscellaneous Expenses & Losses (if any))

Some analysts also calculate Return on Capital Employed (ROCE) as follows:

$$\text{ROCE} = \frac{\text{PAT} + \text{Interest}}{\text{Total Capital Employed}}$$

Total Capital Employed
= Fixed Assets − Capital Work in Progress + (Current Assets − Current Liabilities)

Liquidity ratio

This ratio is a measure of the firm's ability to meet its current commitments as and when they become due. **An ideal figure is 1.33:1**

(i) **Current Ratio**

$$\text{Current Ratio} = \frac{\text{Current Assets}}{\text{Current Liabilities}}$$

(ii) **Quick Ratio**

$$\text{Quick Ratio (or) Acid Test Ratio} = \frac{\text{Current Assets - Inventory}}{\text{Current Liabilities}}$$

This ratio highlights the effect of overstocking. **Ideally this ratio should be 1:1**

This is a relative measure and is best compared with industry average. In the Automotive Sector, Negative Net Current Assets is also a possibility. Eg. TATA Motors Limited, Hero Honda Limited.

This is because these companies command better brand value and hence secure payment in advance for supply of their goods. This together with effective TQM, JIT, KAIZEN and other interventions and a rational credit policy with Business Partners who supply goods and services can keep investment in Net Current Asset quite low or even negative.

solvency ratio

i) $\text{Debt Equity Ratio} = \dfrac{\text{Total Outside Liabilities (LoanFunds)}}{\text{Share Holders Funds}} \text{ Times}$

ii) $\text{Interest Coverage Ratio} = \dfrac{\text{PAT} + \text{Interest}}{\text{Interest}} \text{ Times}$

iii) $\text{Asset Cover} = \dfrac{\text{Total Assets(Including Investments}}{\text{Total Outside Liabilities}}$

[Total Assets = Fixed Assets + (Current Assets − Current Liability) + Investments]

These are measures of the company's financial leverage. More debt does not necessarily indicate a Solvency risk so long as the company's Return on Investment is well above its Weighted Average Cost of capital. This ratio is usually computed by bankers and lenders.

Market test ratios

$$\text{Earnings Per Share (EPS)} = \frac{\text{Profit After Tax}}{\text{No. of Equity Shares}}$$

$$\text{Price Earnings Ratio (PE)} = \frac{\text{Market Price}}{\text{EPS}}$$

The Price Earnings multiple is compared with industry average or competitor. The lower the PE Multiple, the more attractive the share is as a potential investment.

Chapter 10: Understanding Financial Plan

"Do not worry about your difficulties in Mathematics. I can assure you mine are still greater."

Albert Einstein (1879–1955)
US (German-born) Physicist

We have explored accounting from the point of view of a chartered accountant. Now we will see how an entrepreneur looks at it.

Most of us entrepreneurs hate finance just like what Albert Einstein said. Do not worry, we are worse off than you in financial planning. We are going to make finance as simple as it can get. When you finish this chapter you would have a good understanding on financial plan without getting a degree in finance.

Why A FinAnciAL PLAn?

It will help one manage better. To show your lenders and investors that you have done your homework. A financial plan has three components, namely (1) Basic Financial Reports, (2) Breakeven Point Analysis and (3) Ratio Analysis. Now let us take a look at each of these components.

FinAnciAL rePort

Basic Financial Report has three major reports: (i) balance sheet, (ii) income statement and (iii) cash flow.

balance sheet

Provides a company's worth on a given date. It is Assets = Liability + Owner's equity. Assets are current, fixed and intangible. Current assets are short term i.e. less than. one year. This includes cash in bank, items which can be converted into cash within one year, (that is account receivable) and inventory less bad debts. Fixed assets are long term i.e. more than one year. These include land and building less depreciation. Intangible assets are copyright, patent, trademark and goodwill.

Liabilities are current and long term. Current liability is short term, that is less than one year. These include accounts payable, note payable, wages, taxes etc. Long term, that is more than one year and include mortgage and long term note payable.

Owner's equity is investment by the investors.

> - A 10 % increase or decrease on one side is reciprocated on the other side.

income statement

Income statement is also known as profit and loss (P & L) statement. The purpose of this statement is to compare expense against revenue over a period of time. Profit or loss is the difference between revenue and expenses.

cash flow statement

Cash flow statement shows the change in business working capital. To do this, we first need the balance sheet and income statement and then the source of funds. Please note depreciation is considered as a source of fund.

Total expense against total source is the increase or decrease of working capital.

breAK-eVen Point AnALysis

Break-even point indicates the minimum level of sales required to break-even. It provides a good indication but it is too simple to use as a final method because it ignores cash flow.

rAtio AnALysis

Ratio analysis compares significant numbers from the financial statement. Each ratio indicator depends on the business you are in. This is probably the most difficult part to understand in finance. We have attempted to keep it simple and we believe we have succeeded in doing so.

There are 4 main ratios and each in turn have other ratios

- Liquidity Ratios
    - Indicates company's ability to pay its bills
- Leverage Ratios
    - Finances supplied by owner against creditors
- Operating Ratios
    - For evaluating performances of the company
- Profitability Ratios
    - Indicates how well a company is managed

Liquidity ratios

There are three ratios under this i.e. current, quick and cash ratio. They are all the same except that the stringentness increases from the first to the third. The higher the ratio, the better you are placed in paying back your liabilities.

- **Current ratio or working capital ratio**

    Equal to Current assets divided by current liability e.g. 2000/1000 = 2 (indicates for every Rs. 2 of asset it has Re. 1 of liability)

- **Quick ratio or acid ratio**

    Equal to quick assets divided by current liability e.g. 1500/1000 = 1.5 (indicates for every Rs. 1.50 of asset it has Re. 1 of liability. This is a more rigorous test.)

- **Cash ratio**

    Equal to cash divided by current liability e.g. 1000/1000 = 1 (indicates for every Re. 1 of asset it has Re. 1 of liability. This is the most rigorous test.)

Leverage ratios

Again there are three ratios under this. Debt, Debt-to-net worth and Times interest earned ratio. The first two are the same except that the stringentness increases from the first to the second. A lower ratio of these two indicates little borrowing. A high ratio of the third indicates that the company has no problem in paying back loans by itself.

- **Debt ratio**

    Equal to total debt or liabilities divided by total assets. A small ratio indicates that most of the financing is done by the company.

- **Debt-to-net worth ratio**

- Equal to total debt or liabilities divided by tangible net worth. Again this is a more rigorous test.

- **Times interest earned ratio**

    Equal to earning before tax and interest divided by total interest expense. A higher ratio indicates the company has little problem to pay the interest.

operating ratios

Here there are five ratios. Under this ratio, indicate how efficiently a company is operating.

- **Average Inventory Turnover Ratio**

    Equal to cost of goods sold divided by average inventory and average inventory is equal to inventory at the beginning of period plus inventory at the end of that period divided by two. This indicates how well the inventory is managed.

- **Average Collection Period Ratio**

    Equal to days in an accounting period divided by receivable turnover ratio and receivable turnover ratio is equal to credit sales divided by accounts receivable. This indicates how well the company is managing its collections.

- **Average Payable Period Ratio**

    Equal to days in an accounting period divided by payable turnover ratio and payable turnover ratio is equal to purchases divided by account payable. This indicates how well the company is managing to pay its creditors.

- **Net Sales to total Assets Ratio**

    Equal to net sales divided by total assets. This indicates how well the company is doing against other companies. A ratio below others indicates that it is not doing as well as others.

- **Net Sales to Working Capital Ratio**

    Equals to net sales divided by working capital. Working capital is the difference between current assets and liabilities. This indicates how well the company is using its working capital. A low value shows that the company is not applying its working capital efficiently.

Profitability ratios

Here there are two ratios. Under this, ratio indicates how efficiently a company is managed.

- **Net Profit on Sales Ratio or Profit Margin on sales**

    Equals to net profit divided by net sales revenue. This indicates how successful the company is. A higher value is required.

- **Net Profit to Equity Ratio**

    Equal to net profit divided by owner's equity. This indicates the return on the owner's equity. A lower value may indicate that the equity should be employed elsewhere.

MAnAGinG cAsh FLoW

A healthy cash flow is an essential part of any successful business. Failure to have enough cash to pay your suppliers, creditors, or your employees implies that you're out of business! Proper management of your cash flow is very important in making your business successful.

unDerstAnDinG cAsh FLoW

In its simplest form, cash flow is the movement of money in and out of your business. It can be described as the process in which your business uses cash to generate goods or services for the sale to your customers, collects the cash from the sales, and then completes this cycle all over again.

Why is it important to manage cash flow? Smart cash flow management is vital to the health of your business. Hopefully, each time through the cycle, a little more money is put back into the cash flow cycle than which flows out. Your profit is not the same as your cash flow. It's possible to show a healthy profit at the end of the year, and yet face a significant money squeeze at various points during the year.

To properly manage your business' cash flow, you must first analyze the components that affect the timing of your cash inflows and outflows. A good analysis of these components will point out the problem areas that lead to cash flow gaps in your business. Narrowing or even closing cash flow gaps is the key to cash flow management.

Important components to examine are:
- The accounts receivable which is the money people owe you.
- The credit terms, are the time allowed before you pay or others pay you.
- The credit policy which details the credit terms for your company.
- The inventory which is the stock you have.
- The accounts payable which is the money you owe others.

cAsh FLoW buDGet

A cash flow budget is a projection of your business' cash inflows and outflows over a certain period of time. A typical cash flow budget predicts the anticipated cash receipts and disbursements of a business on a month-to-month basis.

At least a six-month cash flow budget has to be prepared in advance. The primary purpose of using a cash flow budget is to predict your business' ability to take in more cash than it pays out. The cash flow budget can also predict your business' cash flow gaps — periods when cash outflows exceed cash inflows when combined with your cash reserves. You can take cash flow management steps to ensure that the gaps are closed, or atleast narrowed, when they are predicted early.

Preparing a cash flow budget involves four steps:
- Preparing a sales forecast
- Projecting your anticipated cash inflows
- Projecting your anticipated cash outflows
- Consolidating the projections together to come up with your cash flow bottomline

You can improve your cash flow in the following ways:
- Improve the flow of money into your business
- Delay the flow of money out of your business
- Reduce the amounts you pay for operational costs of your business

How to fill cash flow gaps? Cash outflows and inflows rarely, if ever, occur at the same time. More often than not, cash inflows lag behind your cash outflows, leaving your business short of money on occasions. Some cash flow gaps are created intentionally.

Cash flow gaps are often filled by external financing sources.

What to do with a Cash Surplus? Managing and improving your cash flow should result in a cash surplus for your business. A cash surplus is the cash that exceeds the cash required for day-to-day operations. How you handle your cash surplus is just as important as the management of money in and out of your company. Two of the most common uses of extra cash are paying debts and making investment.

P<small>Art iii</small>

Entrepreneurial Drive: Marketing

Chapter 11 — Entrepreneurial Marketing

"Whatever you do is just like a bowler in a cricket match; he must bowl to bowl out the opponent."

Muthu Singaram, 2004

Marketing is probably the most important activity of your venture. Unfortunately most of us are not well equipped in this area. It is worth spending your time to explore and learn marketing well before embarking on your venture.

Marketing Plan must integrate various marketing components to create customer value. In order to have a marketing plan you do not need to be a large company. A plan will help you to maintain or gain market share, show your innovation and improve the company's position.

WhAt is MArKetinG?

Marketing is a series of activities carried out to find out what your customers (both existing and prospective) need or want. You should apply all your efforts in the business towards making sure your customers get what they need or want. By doing this you will be able to meet their expectations or exceed them.

Trends are always changing. So you need to keep your eyes on your customers to see what is changing. This can be done by doing something as simple as watching television. It is absolutely important that you keep doing research. You can only stop doing research if your business will grow on momentum with no improvement, you know all about your competitors, you cannot lose customers, your products would not go obsolete, no trend changes, you are the only one with ideas, you can tell the future, you know tomorrow's requirement yesterday, you have billions worth of contract.

Research can be done in two ways. One primary and the other secondary research. Primary research is when you collect data which no one has and in secondary research you use data available to conduct your research. The cost of primary research is much higher. So we might need to use secondary research to reduce cost when you start out. The good news is that with the internet, secondary research virtually comes free or with minimal cost. So you have no excuse not to do research.

A good research can help you in the following ways:
- Show ways to increase the off-peak or off-season business.
- Show ways to increase the customers' spending patterns.
- Show ways to ensure that the customers keep coming back.

MArKetinG strAteGies

Can you list atleast 10 things your potential customer needs or wants? Have you taken any personal action to market yourself and your venture? To help answer these you can apply the famous 4Ps of marketing known as marketing mix.

The 4Ps are product, price, placement and promotion. Now look at these Ps to promote yourself and venture. Sometime these 4Ps and 3 more Ps are known as 7Ps. These 3Ps are people, process and physical evidence. With technology these 4Ps can be looked at from a different angle penetration, permission, personalization, and profitability. Once you have done these you are ready to write your marketing plan.

Product: The product aspects of marketing deal with the specifications of the actual goods or services, and how it relates to the end-user's needs and wants. The scope of a product generally includes supporting elements such as warranties, guarantees and support.

Pricing: This refers to the process of setting a price for a product, including discounts. The price need not be monetary; it can simply be what is exchanged for the product or services, e.g. time, energy or attention.

Placement or distribution: This refers to how the product gets to the customer; for example, point-of-sale placement or retailing. This third P has also sometimes been called Place, referring to the channel by which a product or service is sold (e.g. online vs. retail), which geographic region or industry, to which segment (young adults, families, business people), etc. also referring to how the environment in which the product is sold in can affect sales.

Promotion: Branding refers to the various methods of promoting the product, brand, or company. Advertising, sales promotion, including promotional education, publicity, and personal selling are all methods of branding.

Entrepreneurs conduct research to support marketing activities. The marketing research process spans a number of stages including the definition of a problem, development of a research plan, collecting and interpretation of data and disseminating information formally in the form of a report. The task of marketing research is to provide management with relevant, accurate, reliable, valid and current information.

A distinction should be made between **marketing research** and **market research**. Market research pertains to research in a given market. As an example, a firm may conduct research in a target market, after selecting a suitable market segment. In contrast, marketing research relates to all research conducted within marketing. Thus, market research is a subset of marketing research.

Every entrepreneur has to look into some of the common mixes and matches.

4C's OF MARKETING

The four 'C' model of marketing mix is more consumer-oriented and attempts to fit the movement from 'mass marketing' to 'niche marketing'. The four 'c's are:

Consumer

The product part of four 'p' model is replaced by consumer or consumer model shifting the focus on satisfying the consumer needs.

Cost

Pricing is replaced by cost reflecting the total cost of ownership.

Convenience

Place is replaced by convenience. With the rise of internet and hybrid models of purchasing, place is becoming less relevant. It takes into account the ease of buying product, finding information about the product and several other factors.

Communication

Promotion is replaced by communication which represents broader focus. Communications can include advertising, public relations, personal selling.

4A's MARKETING

Acceptance

You must not emphasise on the product, we must be more focussed on "acceptance". A niche market is not enough; you have to market for the niche who are willing to pay counts.

Availability

The brand mantra here is "Jo dikhta hai Wo Bikhta" i.e the product should be available in the market and so consumers can get the product.

Awareness

You should focus on awareness rather than promotion. The rule here should be "Advertising must be in right proportion, like salt" i.e making the consumers aware about our product in the market. This shift in the mindset could help save money.

Affordability

You should focus on affordability, ensure that the product available in the market is affordable by the consumers.

PRODUCT MIX

Product mix is about the combination of products manufactured or traded by your company to reinforce your presence in the market in order to increase market share to increase the turnover for more profitability. Usually the product mix should have synergy with other products for your medium size organization but when you are in large groups you may have diversified products within the core competency

ProDuct strAteGy MiX

	Existing Products	New Products
	Market Penetration Strategy	**Product Development Strategy**
Existing markets	1. More purchase and usage from existing customers 2. Gain customers from competitors 3. Convert non-users into users	1. Product modification via new features 2. Different quality levels 3. 'New' product
	Market Development Strategy	**Diversification Strategy**
New Markets	1. New market segments 2. New distribution channels 3. New geographic areas	1. Organic growth 2. Joint ventures 3. Mergers 4. Acquisition/take-overs

the AnsoFF MAtriX

Market segmentation, targeting and positioning

Segmentation, targeting and positioning are processes used to gain market share by creating an advantage in the market. These will assist a company to differentiate its products or services from that of its competitors and help it reach the intended market.

Market segmentation is the process of looking at the market for similar groups according to the characteristics intended for the product. Targeting is the process of looking for the most suitable market segments for the product. Positioning is the process of definitive marketing strategy to be applied to reach the market.

Market segmentation

"Market segmentation" is more than psychographics, lifestyles, values, behaviors of the customers' routines.

Market segmentation should be looked at a much broader concept but unfortunately most businesses throughout the world miss this concept. The reason for segmentation is so that the business can concentrate its marketing energy and force on the subdivided (or that market segment) in order to have a competitive advantage.

When a group of people or organizations with one or more characteristics that makes them want a similar product or services based on qualities of those products such as price or function, we would have created a segment. Then these people make up a real market segment that meets all criteria and will be unique from other segments and this is homogeneous within the segment and we can then reach this market. The market segmentation can be based on gender, price interests, culture etc. In theory there may be an 'ideal' market segment but in reality every organization will need to develop different ways of creating market segments. Improving segmentation can lead to marked improved marketing effectiveness. This is the way how you can apply greater marketing energy or force to a market segment. A great deal of money is wasted in this area and it leads to no great advantage. So an entrepreneur should focus in the segment for their products and services.

Targeting

Once we have segmented, we now need to target a group of customers. We need to see how many others are serving this group. If there is already a large number of others serving these customers it would be more difficult to penetrate this group.

If not many are serving then the next stage is to see how large the segment is and the potential growth bearing in mind that a fast growing product or service would attract competition. Then do we have strengths which we can use to appeal to the potential customers against the bigger names.

Positioning

Once we have targeted the segment now we need to implement that target. The most important lesson for an entrepreneur is learning how to transform your passion into position. Good positioning helps to put your products and services in the minds of potential customers. Every day we as individuals are continuously trying to position ourselves example to be the best in the class, great at numbers or smart. These create an image for us and hence we are able to position ourselves in the society.

Primarily positioning allows you to create an image in the market. We all need to create an image in order to be who we want to be, doing what we want to do and having what you want to have.

Positioning your products and services can lead to great success. If someone else positions you then your choices are limited and hence your opportunities. That is why it is crucial for entrepreneurs to transform their passion into a market position. You should define your product or service otherwise a competitor will do it for you.

BCG growth-share matrix

The BCG matrix was developed by Bruce Henderson of the Boston consulting Group in the early 1970's. The BCG matrix is a good portfolio management tool used in product life cycle theory. BCG matrix is often used to prioritize which products get more funding and attention.

The BCG model is based on classification of products on market growth and market share relative to the biggest competitor into four categories.

Each stage of a product's or service's life-cycle provides a different profile of risk and return. A company should have a well balanced portfolio of products and services both in high-growth as well as in low-growth.

High-growth is a new product where you would require high resources and a low-growth is an old product where you would require low resources. A company needs to focus on both these areas.

The question here is how do we know which phase is our product or services and how do we classify what we are to sell? The BCG matrix helps us to make a decision as to which product to focus on.

The matrix looks beyond product mix. It also looks at the sales and this would help us make decisions on what priorities to be given not only to products but also to other aspects like departments and business units.

cash cow

These are products or services with high market share in a slow growing industry. These generate excess cash and low to maintain the business. All of us want as many of these so that we can continue to milk with little investment.

Dogs

These are products or services with low market share in a slow growing industry. These are generally breaking even barely generating enough cash to maintain market share. These are usually continued for social benefits or to help other units.

Question Marks

These are products or services with low growth and market share and use up large amounts of cash. However, a question mark can turn to a star and then to a cow depending on market movement.

stars

These are products or services with high growth and market share. The hope is that these would become cash cows in due course of time. Sometime large amount of cash is required to stay as market leaders. When growth slows down these become cash cows.

Chapter 12

Entrepreneurial Marketing Research

"Whatever you do is just like a bowler in a cricket match; he must bowl to bowl out the opponent."

Muthu Singaram, 2004

Market Research is a systematic and logical process which you would use in your effort to gather information about markets or customers you want to target. It is a critical element of your business strategy. Market research is primarily used to find out what people want, need and desire. It can be used to obtain a detailed study about the behavioural pattern of the customers whom you are looking for by discovering how they act and react.

You must understand that market research and marketing research are used interchangeably more often than not but there is a fine line of distinction between the two. When you do a marketing research it is concerned specifically about marketing processes, while market research is concerned specifically with markets.

MethoDs oF MArKet reseArch

There are many ways to perform market research. Most entrepreneurs apply one or more of the five basic methods of market research which are surveys, focus groups, personal interviews, observation and field trials.

Depending on the type of data you require and the finance available you will determine which techniques an entrepreneur chooses for his business.

You, as an entrepreneur, nothing beats talking directly with the customers, it can be your existing customers or potential customers. There are many aspects of consumer behaviour that cannot be extracted by using technology alone. It is always something great about connecting with a real human being who reveals intricacies which research alone cannot bring up. The technical touch research is used primarily for analytical and linear solutions. The human touch research is a more relational and holistic approach. The focus with the human touch research is to understand better directly from the market what the customers want. You as an entrepreneur must apply both human touch and technology based research to get valuable information which will help you create a winning business and product.

WAys to Do huMAn touch reseArch

The best way to find out what the market wants is to ask the customers what they want and this should be done in person. A face to face encounter would give you a chance to determine how passionate the customer is with your product and their willingness to pay for your product.

It is worth noting that direct contact would reveal a lot but there are chances that they may not want to really expose the full precision of what's going on for them because they may not even know. Another way to learn about the market is by interviewing people who know your target market well. These can be business colleagues or associates. These are people who could give an objective third person point of view about the market. These people would know personally what's going on in the minds of the customer.

These factors should be taken into consideration while carrying out a market research.

Market information

You need market information to learn about your competitors i.e., the prices of products in the market, and availability and demand situation. This information about the markets can be obtained from different sources, varieties and formats to make your business work.

Market segmentation

You must look at market segmentation i.e., which division of the market or population who have similar motivations to buy your product. Generally segmentation is done on geographic differences, personality differences, demographic differences, technographic differences, use of product differences, psychographic differences and gender differences.

Market trends

Market trends tell you during which period of time there is upward or downward movements of a market. It is difficult to predict the market size if you are starting with something completely new. Here you will have to derive the figures from the number of potential customers, or customer segments.

Besides information about the target market you need information about who your competitors, customers, products, etc are. Last but most important, you need to measure your marketing effectiveness by using series of techniques like customer analysis, choice modelling, competitor analysis, risk analysis, product research, advertising research, marketing mix modelling, etc.

Chapter 13

Entrepreneurial Marketing plan

"Just like playing cricket, a batsman must want to run to win."

Muthu Singaram, 2004

Every marketing plan must have four elements— personality, budget, business and time.

A typical marketing plan's main contents are:

1. Executive Summary
2. Situational Analysis
3. Opportunities / Issue Analysis - SWOT Analysis
4. Objectives
5. Strategy
6. Action Programme
7. Financial Forecast
8. Controls

coMPeLte MArKetinG PLAn

1. title page

2. executive summary

3. current situation - Macroenvironment
- Economy
- Legal
- Government
- Technology
- Ecological
- Sociocultural
- Supply chain

4. **current situation - Market Analysis**
   - Market definition
   - Market size
   - Market segmentation
   - Industry structure and strategic groupings
   - Porter 5 forces analysis
   - Competition and market share
   - Competitors' strengths and weaknesses
   - Market trends

5. **current situation - consumer Analysis**
   - Nature of the buying decision
   - Participants
   - Demographics
   - Psychographics
   - Buyer motivation and expectations
   - Loyalty segments

6. **current situation - internal**
   - Company resources
   - Financial
   - People
   - Time
   - Skills
   - Objectives
   - Mission statement and vision statement
   - Corporate objectives
   - Financial objectives
   - Marketing objectives
   - Long-term objectives
   - Description of the basic business philosophy
   - Corporate culture

7. **summary of situation Analysis**
   - External threats
   - External opportunities

- Internal strengths
- Internal weaknesses
- Critical success factors in the industry
- Our sustainable competitive advantage

8. **Marketing research**
   - Information requirements
   - Research methodology
   - Research results

9. **Marketing strategy - Product**
   - Product mix
   - Product strengths and weaknesses
   - Perceptual mapping
   - Product life cycle management and new product development
   - Brand name, brand image and brand equity
   - The augmented product
   - Product portfolio analysis
   - B.C.G. analysis
   - Contribution margin analysis
   - G.E. Multi Factoral analysis
   - Quality function deployment

10. **Marketing strategy-segmented Marketing Actions and Market share objectives**
    - By product
    - By customer segment
    - By geographical market
    - By distribution channel

11. **Marketing strategy—Price**
    - Pricing objectives
    - Pricing method (e.g.: cost plus, demand based, or competitor indexing)
    - Pricing strategy (e.g.: skimming, or penetration)
    - Discounts and allowances
    - Price elasticity and customer sensitivity

- Price zoning
- Break even analysis at various prices

12. Marketing strategy—Promotion

- Promotional goals
- Promotional mix
- Advertising reach, frequency, flights, theme and media
- Sales force requirements, techniques and management
- Sales promotion
- Publicity and public relations
- Electronic promotion (e.g.: Web, or telephone)
- Word of mouth marketing (buzz)
- Viral marketing

13. Marketing strategy—Distribution

- Geographical coverage
- Distribution channels
- Physical distribution and logistics
- Electronic distribution

14. implementation

- Personnel requirements
- Assign responsibilities
- Give incentives
- Training on selling methods
- Financial requirements
- Management information systems requirements
- Month-by-month agenda
- PERT or critical path analysis
- Monitoring results and benchmarks
- Adjustment mechanism
- Contingencies (What if's)

15. Financial summary

- Assumptions
- Pro-forma monthly income statement
- Contribution margin analysis

- Break-even analysis
- Monte Carlo method
- ISI: Internet Strategic Intelligence

16. scenarios

- Prediction of future scenarios
- Plan of action for each scenario

17. Appendix

- Pictures and specifications of the new product
- Results from research already completed

The content is captured from wikepedia http://www.wikipedia.org/. I have used this because I feel it is very well captured and any attempt to rewrite is a waste of time.

Now use methods which you are comfortable in applying, look for methods which are easiest and cost effective to access specific people you want to reach and do not depend only on one method at a time. Apply, activities that complement one another and check your methods against your competitors, methods and find out what is working well for them. You must track the outcome of your marketing efforts.

Please note that you can increase your business only in these three ways (i) by increasing the number of clients, (ii) increasing size of the sale per client and (iii) increasing the number of times clients return and buy. With these in mind now ask yourself these questions:

- What is the number of clients you have?
- How much do these clients spend on an average on each transaction?
- How often do these clients buy from you?

Now let us look at an example

Let us say you have 100 clients. Each buy for Rs.100 each time and buys twice a year. Your revenue is 100 * Rs.100 * 2 which equals to Rs.20000. Now you want to increase your revenue by 20 % that is Rs.24000. So you need to have more clients, bigger sales from your existing clients for each sale or increase in the frequency of buying. Once you have this worked out your sales can easily increase.

How do we increase these? By creating a desire for the client to use our services and product. Here we can apply *Maslow's hierarchy of needs* to our product and services. Maslow says that there are five levels of needs. These are physiological needs which include basic needs like food, clothing, sex, shelter, etc, safety needs so you do not feel threatened, social needs to have a sense of belonging, esteem needs to have self esteem and recognition and self-actualization needs which include self-development, creativity and psychological health.

MuLti-LeVeL MArKetinG (MLM) AnD FrAnchisinG

These are the two biggest marketing activities discovered in the last century. Both have tremendous potential for accelerated growth.

Multi-level marketing (MLM)

Also known as **Network Marketing**. In this model individuals or companies are allowed by a parent company to market its products directly to consumers by means of direct selling and referrals.

Usually individuals act as unsalaried sales people of multi-level marketing and are referred to as distributors. They represent the company and are given a commission based on the volume of products sold by them.

Each distributor develops his or her own organization either by building an active customer base to whom they sell directly from the parent company or by recruiting a downline of distributors who in turn build a customer base, thereby expanding the overall organization. To top their income, distributors can also earn a profit by retailing products they purchased from the parent company at wholesale price.

Distributors earn commission for the overall organizations they build based on sales of individuals and group, based on the compensation plan designed by the parent company.

Franchising

It refers to the methods of practising and using someone else's idea to do business. The franchisor, the owner, gives the rights to an independent operator or franchisee the right to distribute its products, techniques, and use its trademarks for a percentage on gross monthly sales and / or royalty fee for an agreed period of time.

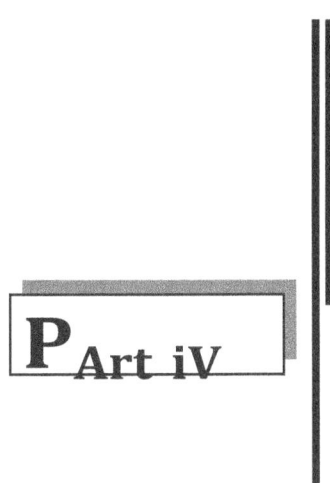

Part iV

Entrepreneurial Planning

Chapter 14

Entrepreneurial Business Plan

"You see things; and you say, 'Why?' But I dream things that never were; and I say, 'Why not?'."

George Bernard Shaw (1856–1950)
Irish dramatist & socialist

Why a business plan for an entrepreneur? The reason is, it defines your business, identifies your goals and serves as your firm's resume. The business plan should include a current and proforma balance sheet, an income statement, and a cash flow analysis. Additionally, it informs sales personnel, suppliers, and others about your operations and goals.

the iMPortAnce oF A business PLAn

The importance of a comprehensive business plan is that much depends on it for outside funding, credit from suppliers, management of your operation and finances, promotion and marketing of your business and achievement of your goals and objectives.

Before writing your business plan ask yourself the following:

- What service or product does your business provide and what needs does it fulfil?
- Who are the potential customers for your product or service and why will they purchase it from you?
- How will you reach your potential customers?
- Where will you get the financial resources to start your business?

Now that you have the answers, you can start with your plan. Your plan should include a description of the business, a marketing plan, financial plan and management team.

coMPonents oF A business PLAn

A typical business plan should include the following:

- Executive Summary
- Company Direction
- Company Operations
- Products/Services

- Market Analysis
- Marketing Plan
- Financial Plan
- Supporting Documents

This is not the only format but generally most business plans will follow some sort of outline similar to this. Now let us take a look at each of these one by one.

executive summary

An executive summary is the summary of the entire business plan and comes at the start of the business plan. This will summarize in 1 to 2 pages what the business plan is about. So this will give the reader a chance to see if he is excited enough to read the whole plan. For this very reason you must ensure it is written well. There are two schools of thought, viz., you can write the executive summary at the start or at the end of preparing your business plan. Some say if you do not know what you are going to write then how can you write the plan. So they suggest you to do the summary first. Others say you can summarise in the end once you have completed the business plan.

> I feel that both have merits and demerits. So you should select whichever option you are comfortable with.

company Direction

The first chapter in the business plan is the company direction. This should cover in detail the present situation, vision, mission, goals and objectives.

In this you are telling the reader what you have done so far and the status of your project. You should also cover your vision in what you hope to achieve in the long term, the mission is what you are going to do to achieve your vision, goals are long term achievement more than one year and must be quantified and objectives are short term and again must be quantified.

company operations

Here you should talk about the legal business description, that is, what type of structure you have decided to use, as detailed on chapter 4. As explained, there are two components for this. They are (i) the team members and (ii) the legal status of your company. The team members fall under management team, board of directors and staffing.

All three have different functions. Therefore, here you should only speak about relevance to your business. The management team is the one which will manage the business on a day-to-day basis. The board of directors are the ones who set the company directions. The staffs are the ones who actually carry out all the actions. Strategic alliances are outsiders with whom you have made some arrangements to enhance your business. These can be vendors, support service and really anything that can help you achieve your vision.

Products/services

Here you have descriptions for all your products/services. You must also address how you are positioning your products/services in the marketplace. It is important to have a competitive evaluation of products/services. All future products/services should also be discussed here but you must be cautious that you do not overdo it and sound like you are only concentrating on new products and not on making money.

Market Analysis

Market analysis is different from a marketing plan. First, you need to carry out a market analysis and then write the plan. The market analysis should include the market definition where you define what the market means to your business then your customer profile as to who will be the ones you have defined that you will serve next who will be your competition for these customers and finally the risk in doing this business. Once you have addressed these, you are now ready to write the plan.

Marketing Plan

This is the plan as to how you are going to get your customers. A detailed marketing plan was discussed in marketing chapter. This will include the marketing strategies like, sales tactics, advertising, promotions / incentives, publicity and trade shows.

Financial Plan

This will be the cost and pricing of your products and services. Again this was covered in detail in the chapter on finance. This will include assumptions, financial statements, capital requirements, use of funds, exit / payback strategy and conclusion.

supporting Documents

This is a section which will include details of anything which will support your business plan. In the earlier chapter on finance we just included very large figures, like an overview but here, there should be detailed calculations and you must include resumes of key personnel.

Now how can you use your business plan? There are three areas where you can use it.

(i) Almost every unit in a company should have a business plan where they use it to communicate with their colleagues and for others to see what they are doing.

(ii) For the management to know what your team is trying to do or achieve.

(iii) It is a very good planning tool which actually tells you things which you would not have known otherwise. The fact that you have actually written them down will enable you to find things which otherwise you would have never come across. It is actually a survival plan.

Now how can you get help to identify these plans?. There are plenty of books in the book shops which you can read and write the business plan yourself. There are actually business plan software tools that you can use to develop your own business plan. There are also business plan websites which do business plans for you. And finally, there are many big organizations who use professional business plan services. For a start you probably don't have enough money. You probably have to do the business plan yourself. And I personally believe it is probably better for you to do your own business plan because nobody knows what you hope to achieve in your business over the next 12 months, 36 months and 60 months. As you are the one who is most involved with your own business it is better for you to come up with your own business plan.

Entrepreneurial Power Presentation

Chapter 15

"Dreams come true. Without that possibility, nature would not incite us to have them."

John Updike (1932–2009)
US author

Once you have completed your business plan you will need to prepare a presentation to present your idea to others. This is known as a Power presentation.

the objectives of A PoWer PresentAtion

- Your "task" is to hold the attention of the audience long enough to make your "point". Not the transmission but the reception.
- The presentation must be geared towards the audience and not towards the speaker.
- Often, good projects fail because the audience are either not persuaded of its worth or do not understand the project.
- The presentation is to make your message understandable and memorable.
- The main challenge in achieving these objectives is that the average audience has a very short span of attention and would be thinking about a million other things at the same time.

WhAt cAn A PoWer PresentAtion Do For you?

Firstly, it gives you and your team a chance to show your skill and ability in order to obtain the resources that you require. Secondly, it gives you a chance to raise issues, present problems or at least to establish, who, amongst the audience could provide valuable input to help. Finally, it is fun and a chance to network with others.

the coMPonents of A PoWer PresentAtion

Planning, Preparation and Delivery.

The Planning Phase

Working hard to gather material.

- Using the material to identify your central theme.
- Develop each point to support the central theme.
- Organize the content.

The Preparation Phase

Taking the substance of your presentation and bringing it to life.

- By structuring it in accordance with power presentation.
- By further enlivening it with humour, quotations, analogies, anecdotes and other tools.

The Delivery Phase

Presenting it to an audience.

- Use of unique personal style.
- Use of audio/visuals (if any).

bAsic GuiDeLines

Preparing Your Presentation

> List the top three things that you want to accomplish. You must be clear with what you want to accomplish and understand the audience. Make sure the audience understand what you are trying to accomplish. Explain the flow of the presentation. Spend 25 minutes on the main presentation. Spend 5 minutes to finish up. Be prepared for 15 minutes of Question and Answer session.

Preparing Your Presentation

You might be handing out supplemental materials i.e., articles, reports, or copies of your presentation. You will use a personal computer onto a projection screen so check the slides before hand. Use presentable slides.

Spend 2-5 minutes on each slide limiting each to 5-8 lines of bulleted phrases. If you want to give the audience any material, do it at the end so that when you are presenting, they will listen to you and not read it. If you are handing out your presentation make sure it is readable and there is space for them to make notes. Speak louder and slower than usual. You can practice by sitting in front of a mirror. Do not be monotonous. Vary your speed and volume. Stand firmly and keep your hands relatively still.

A typical power presentation will contain the following slides:

Introduction and Overview

- Title of the project
- What are you looking for?
- What business are you in?

Elevator pitch

- 30 to 45 second pitch with the essence of your business plan

Make it short and simple
Concentrate
- What is the burning problem?
- How big is the opportunity?
- What is so unique?
- So what are the benefits?
- What is the mission statement?
- Call to action

Problem Statement
- What problem are you addressing?

Potential Market Size
- What is the market size?

Proposed Solutions
- How does your solution address the problem?

Our Solutions are based on
- What standards are your solutions based on?
- What existing technologies are you going to use?

Technologies—barrier to entry
- Flexibility and scalability
- Reliability and availability
- People-driven technology
- Market determined technology
- Why others cannot do what you are doing?

Competition
- Who are the competitors?
- If none, why?

Marketing and leverage points
- How are you going to market?
- Hire a team?
- Outsource?
- What are your strengths?

Business Models
- Subscription business model
- Razor and blades business model (bait and hook)
- Pyramid scheme business model
- Multi-level marketing business model
- Network effects business model
- Monopolistic business model

- Cutting out the middleman model
- Auction business model
- Online auction business model
- Bricks and clicks business model
- Loyalty business models
- Collective business models
- Industrialization of services business model
- Servitization of products business model
- Low-cost carrier business model
- Online content business model
- Freemium business model
- Premium business model
- Direct sales model
- Value Added Reseller model
- Professional open-source model
- Various distribution business models
- Franchise

Management team
- Who is the CEO?
- Who is the CTO?, etc.
- Here talk about their relevant experiences and qualifications.

Status
- What have you achieved so far?
- Have you raised any money?
- Have you formed any partnership?
- Have you performed pilot testing?
- Do you have any customers?
- Do you have any revenue?

Future Plan
- What are your plans in the future?
- What are you going to do with the money you raise?
- What are the future products and services?
- Who are your management?

Conclusion
- Tell the audience what you want, what you are going to do for them and ask them to commit.

ViscerAL Pitch

Dress smartly

Rely on clothing as a resource, a tool that you can use to grab attention and appeal to the audience or investors or buyers. Clothing has a certain power that affects the way you think, feel, act and the way others react, as visual plays as great role in at triggering emotions.

The two important style features that will grab and maintain the audience's attention, plus stir emotions are Fit and Colour.

Let them see your Passion

A stoic recitation of facts and figures does not engage the audience. What works best is to allow your natural enthusiasm for the company to come across in your vocal tone and emphasis, your physical energy, and your animated expressions. Body language is the prime communication channel of emotion.

Body language is a kind of non-verbal communication where thoughts, intentions or feelings are expressed by physical behaviour, such as gestures, facial expressions, body posture, touch and use of space. According to Albert Mehrabian's study on communication, 55% of what you communicate is through your body language, 38% is paralinguistic and only 7% of what we communicate is through the words we speak.

show confidence and Warmth

From a body language perspective, the most effective "pitchers" send two sets of non-verbal signals. One set of signal conveys status, authority, and confidence. You send these signals by standing tall, holding your shoulders back, keeping your head straight, and speaking clearly in a lower vocal range.

The other set of non-verbal signal conveys warmth, empathy, and like ability. These signals include open palm gestures, leaning slightly forward, giving people eye contact when they talk, smiling, and mirroring their posture/gestures.

Make sure Verbal and non-verbal Messages are Aligned

When your body language doesn't match your words, your verbal message is lost.

Words say one thing and your gestures indicate another, you don't make sense. And if forced to choose between your rhetoric and your body language, people will believe what they see and not what you say.

The challenge while pitching is twofold: First, stressful situations make us behave in ways we are not entirely aware of, and second, we are poor judges of the impression we make on others.

Gauge how you are being Perceived?

In a pitch, engagement and disengagement are the most important signals to monitor your audience's body language. Engagement behaviours indicates interest, receptivity, or agreement while disengagement behaviours signals that a person is bored, angry, or defensive.

Entrepreneurial Strategic Planning

"Strength respects strength"

A. P. J. Abdul Kalam
Former President of India

Now that you have a good understanding of the finance and marketing aspect you can move on to look at the strategic planning for your idea.

> As former President of India said, strength respects strength. This is not only true with strength but with anything. If you are strong iN something people will always respect you.

Under this we will examine the **4 W's and 1 H of Strategy** [what, who, why, when and how].

First W oF strAteGy

What is strategy? A dynamic process involving more than the usual linear sequential planning that is associated with strategic planning.

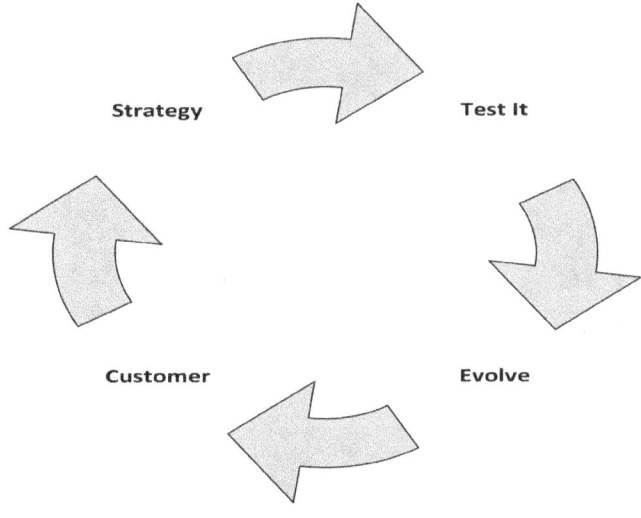

The common mistake about strategy

i) Is that first you plan, then you strategize, then you decide on the tactics.
ii) Strategy is considered the CEO's job.
iii) Strategy comes in a red book.
iv) Strategy comes while you are in the shower.

seconD W oF strAteGy

Who should strategise? Actually everybody in the organization should play a role in strategising.

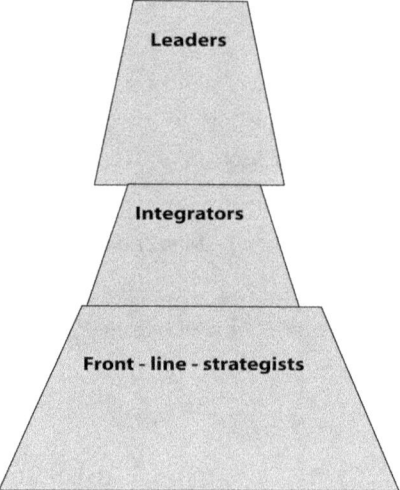

A company will usually have three groups of people. Starting with the front-line strategists, these are the customers, the people who interact with customers and group functional teams. The next level is the integrators. These people connect the front liners and the leaders. They act as the link and tune the strategy and take it to the leaders. In turn the leaders will align these by focusing with company vision and balancing it for the final strategy. As you can see everyone is involved. So when we finalise the strategy no one can say that they were not part of it.

thirD W oF strAteGy

Why strategise? In order to focus on your customers and market needs and the need for staying flexible and responsive to market needs. This is the only way to hold on to valuable and knowledgeable workforce. With a fast paced world, this will avoid management burn out. Strategising is not an option. It is essential to be successful. With technology, things change rapidly, so you need to plan to be ahead of others. Again, planning for a large company is different from planning for a smaller one. Strategising helps you decide how you will compete.

Fourth W oF strAteGy

When strategise? A simple answer and actually the only one is 'all the time'.

h of strategy

How do you strategise? This can come about in two ways (i) listen to customers and (ii) empower your people.

In brief, strategising involves everyone, so strategising takes a lot of time. But if everyone is involved you might ask who makes the decision? That is why we have a leader for each company. How can an organization concentrate if we are chasing our customers for new opportunities? Remember, if customers do not want what we are doing then we lose big time so we need to chase the customer, your BOSS!

the 10 steP PLAnninG Process

1. **Define a clear vision and translate to a meaningful mission.**
   a. Define a vision statement.
   b. Define the mission statement based on the vision.
   c. Mission statement should address the business you are in.
   d. This is the starting point for you and your business.

2. **Define its market position and driving force**
   a. No company can be good at everything. So you need to know what you are good at and work on it.
   b. You need to target a market.
   c. You must be knowledgeable of the market.
   d. Uniqueness of your product.

3. **Determine its strength and weakness**
   a. Once you have identified the market and your driving force you can now assess your strength and weakness.
   b. Strengths are positive internal factors and weaknesses are negative internal factors.

4. **Look at the market for opportunities and threats**
   a. Now identify the opportunities and threats from the market.
   b. Opportunities are positive external factors and threats are negative external factors.

5. **Determine the key success factors**
   a. Every business has controllable variables which determine its success.
   b. These factors can be cost, manufacturing, distribution etc.

6. **Study the competition**
   a. Why study competition?

i. To avoid surprises and to be prepared.
   ii. To identify their threats.
   iii. To improve your planning.
   iv. To understand the market behaviours.

7. **Determine company goals and objectives**
   a. Before embarking on a set of strategies a company must identify its goals and objectives.
   b. Goals are broad long range objectives.
   c. Objectives are short term and more performance specific.
   d. Objectives must be **S**pecific, **M**easurable, **A**ttainable, **R**ealistic, **T**imely (SMART) and 3Ps— Personal, Positive and Put in writing.

8. **Formulate strategy plan**
   a. Formulate and select the strategies.
   b. This is a road map for the company's action to achieve its mission, goals and objectives.
   c. Must be action-oriented.

9. **Define an action plan**
   a. Now translate your strategic plan into an action plan.
   b. No strategic plan is complete until it is put into action.

10. **Monitoring the action plan**
    a. Now check if the plan has produced desired results.
    b. No strategic plan is successful unless we get the desired output.

Now that we have had a look at strategic planning let us move on to look at project management in the next chapter.

Chapter 17

Entrepreneurial Project Management

"Failing to plan is planning to fail"

Robert M Fulmer
Distinguished Visiting Professor at Pepperdine University

WhAt is A ProJect?

A project has a specific timeframe. It is inter-dependent on events with defined outcome and unique characteristics.

A specific timeframe means a temporary undertaking. The timeframe is usually from days to years (usually a maximum of one year). It is worthy to note that all projects must end and have deliverables along the project.

What does interdependent events mean? Projects have a series of events, one event leads to another and sometimes there are multi events. If it is a single event then it is not a project. A project might be so complex, that you might need a software to manage the project. Projects have defined outcome and unique characteristics. At the end of the project there will be something worthwhile. The project will have an end objective but along the way there will be several other objectives to get to this one. Some people call these milestones, phases, tasks or subtasks. Even if you have done a similar project it will always be different every time.

WhAt is ProJect MAnAGeMent?

Project management is a set of principles, methods and techniques used for planning and controlling a project.

Why ProJect MAnAGeMent

We do project management in order to complete on time, within budget, inline with guidelines and objectives. So the project is optimized in time, cost and quality.

history oF ProJect MAnAGeMent

Project management has been around at all ages but started to get recognition in the 1950s. Today it is an important tool in business.

WhAt is GooD ProJect MAnAGeMent

- Be aware of what you are doing.
- Do your homework.
- Be prepared for stumbling blocks.
- Go deep into the problem.
- Be able to change.

hoW to MAnAGe A ProJect?

- Use project management tools.
- Be able to take and give feedback.
- Be open for new ways and ideas.
- Good time management.
- Effective meetings.
- Be able to make decisions.
- Have a sense of humour.

hoW not to MAnAGe A ProJect?

- Not addressing a problem quickly.
- Changing timeline too frequently.
- Ignoring quality to reach milestones.
- Focusing on administration work.
- Micromanaging.
- Using new tools readily.
- Not monitoring regularly.

ProJect PLAnninG

- Preparing a project plan.
- The project plan is the governing document.
- Project methods and resources.
- Project tools.
- Ignoring what people think as a waste of time.
- People spend only 5 % of the time on planning.
- Should spend at least 25 % on planning and rest on execution.
- Planning should be done throughout the project.

eLeMents oF PLAnninG

Problem or opportunity statement.
- Get a clear understanding from your supervisor what is the problem to be solved. Understand their needs and wants. Get background on current status. Understand the motivation of the supervisor for taking this project.

Define objectives.
- Project objectives must be Specific, Measurable, Agreed, Realistic and Timely (SMART) and the Ps.

Write the plan.
- Several times you write the plan and carry out a conceptual review. Is it in line with your objectives? You must be have a Feasibility review. Is it realistic? Benefit-Cost review, is it cost effective? Profitability review, is it profitable? Alternative review is there any other way to do it? Opportunity review, is there any opportunity? Risk review, is there any risk? Outcome review is, to proceed or not?
- Break down these objectives into manageable activities.
- Estimate the time and cost of these activities.
- Do logical sequencing of activities.
  - Bar Charts – Gantt charts.
  - Network Diagrams.
  - Precedence Diagramming Method (PDM) or Activity-on-node.

Calculate the critical path for the project.

Program Evaluation and Review Technique (PERT).
- Provides three estimates.

Mostly (m), Optimistic (o), Pessimistic (p).

Estimated time = $(o + 4m + p)/6$

Critical Path Method (CPM).

Now using the CPM on the network diagram, calculate the critical path.

CPM calculations include Early Start, Late Start, Early Finish, and Late Finish.

Prepare schedules using Gantt Charts.

Crashing schedules happen when there is a change in resources, activities and objectives.

Resource Planning includes identifying skills by recruiting and assigning.

Adjust project schedule.

Get approval for finance.

Set up controls to monitor.

You must have a formal process and not micro manage. Elevate problems to the lowest management in order to ensure being on schedule. You must rank projects

How to set up monitoring and control

Determine information needed. Determine data collection method and frequency.

Start the project

- Formal start off with meeting to agree parameters, roles and other project related activities and communicate to all stakeholders.

Controlling project objectives

- Network diagrams, schedules and budgets are not only for planning but used as control for time, cost, scope, quality and resource.
- Tools used to control are Inspection, Statistical Sampling, Flow charting, Control charts, Trend analysis, Pareto diagrams, Cause and Effect diagrams and Earned Value Analysis.

Reporting Project

- Reports are for communication to others. This can be in graphical reports, reporting percent progressed, sample reporting, status report, schedule, cost and scope.

Take action or re-plan if not in line with original plan.

- During the course of the project there will be minor or major changes. Not all changes are bad. Too many changes may indicate poor planning. Must have formal and regular check for parameter changes i.e., requirement, budget etc.

Project Evaluations.

- Periodic evaluation must be done to ensure accomplishment of the project.
- Project plan is like a map; it tells you where you are.
- Evaluation also motivates the team.
- When to evaluate? On-going reviews, periodic inspections, milestone evaluations and final project audit are all tools for evalution.
- In evaluation, consider quality of work, team performance and project status.

Managing Risk.

- Identify the possible cause. This can be technical, administrative, financial etc.
- You must assess these risks and respond by planning. The possible solution for these risks can be avoiding, transferring, mitigation or accepting the risk.

Close Project.

- Good projects have a formal closure to ensure that the job is done.
- Time to recognize efforts.
- Complete individual, vendor and customer satisfaction evaluation.

ProJect MAnAGeMent soFtWAre

Due to complexity of the project you can use software for Planning, Initiating, Tracking, Monitoring, Reports, Charts and Communication. The following vendors supply project management software — PlanView, Primavera, Microsoft, Dekker, Welcome, Artemus, Quick Gantt, Milestone Simplicity and Project Vision.

Please note that it is beyond the scope or intention of this book to make you a project management expert. You will need to do that by attending a program or buying a book which specializes in project management.

Part V

Entrepreneurial Real and Virtual World of Information

Chapter 18: How Entrepreneurs can Use Technology to Benefit

"Everything that can be invented has been invented."
Charles H. Duell, 1899
Commissioner, U.S. Office of Patents

How wrong Charles H Duell was. Today we have so many technologies at our disposal not only to make our lives better but also to jumpstart our business. In this chapter we will explore a few of these wonderful technologies.

In today's world almost everything is only a click away. It is not only simpler to acquire information but it is freely available using computers, televisions, mobile phones, fax machines, printers, digital cameras, courier services, postal services and the internet.

beneFits oF technoLoGy

Computers can do many of the mundane and replicating jobs without error and are more efficient than humans. Some of the things computers can help us do are accounting, project planning, planning our meetings, translations, research, building a database, word processing, spreadsheets and many more tasks.

Televisions can provide plenty of useful information and promotion for your business. Mobile phones and fax machines allow you to communicate around the world with great ease. Now many businesses have automated telephone system to support their customer service. Printers and digital cameras allow you to produce your material instead of using expensive outsourcing.

Postal and courier services can get your documents and products to their destination overnight, almost anywhere in the world.

> But of all today the biggest and the simplest technologies today, the most helpful is the WONDERFUL internet.

With the advent of the internet many brick and mortar businesses have migrated to another platform as an extension to their business and has generated huge profits. The internet has lead to the formation of many 'e' terms—e-commerce, e-mail, e-tailing, e-service etc.

The '*e*' here means electronic. Most business now have a website and use emails to carry out their business. Telephones, radio, television are all now available on the internet. With this happening more and more business are getting e-ready. What the e-world has enabled for business, other technology has been able to as yet. Surely with us getting smarter and more competitive, some more powerful technology will one day surface.

With the internet you can do most things online; you can do your travel booking, hotel booking, do your shopping and many more things.

However, with all this technology the human touch is somewhat missing but because of the convenience many businesses are moving to these online methods.

It is for us to make a call when to use technology in our work. Technology should work for us and not the other way round.

the internet

With the internet it is virtually impossible for any business not to make use of this great innovation. As we start our business we should maximise the usage of internet and should start with our domain name in relation to our business. It costs less then Rs 500 to purchase a domain. You will need to decide if you want a country level domain or international. Then decide on what extension to the domain. These days there are so many extensions you need to careful to choose your extension. Next, you need to host your website. Again for less than Rs 500 a month you can get a host; some are even free. After this you should create personalised emails and general emails for your business so the outside world can communicate with you and vice versa. You will need to also design your website and this you can do yourself or outsource.

If you are using your website to sell your services and products then you will need a payment gateway in place. However, this can be costly and not everyone can get it. There are other alternatives. One such alternative is Paypal, an online payment site, which allows you to get started without any hassle or cost. With the internet you are able to reach a larger audience with lower cost and shorter time.

When you use technology in your business you must not look at it as cost but should be perceived as an investment.

Email cannot be used as a customer relation management tool. You will need to invest in a true CRM system as this will allow you to keep better track of your customer. It will help you profile your customer and in turn will help your top line.

Another great place you can promote your business is an online community like Facebook where the power of networking is huge.

Mobile technology like the 'blackberry' is a great bonus. You are permanently linked with whoever you choose to and it helps you keep in touch with your customers and suppliers.

You don't have to do, implement or buy technology, you can always outsource to another company. Do not use technology to improve bad practices.

In short technology can be to automate process, access information, analyse information, create specialist systems and improved collaboration.

Chapter 19

Valuable Reading

"Wisdom is a weapon to ward off destruction; It is an inner fortress which enemies cannot destroy."

Thirukkural 421 (200 BC)
Thiruvalluvar, the Tamil Poet

This section is created to help you build your knowledge in various areas because an entrepreneur should be competent.

tiMe AnD eFFiciency

- Covey, Stephen, *First Things First,* 1994.
- Covey, Stephen, *The Seven Habits of Highly Effective People*, 1997.
- Dorff, Pat, *File...Don't Pile*, 1986.
- Douglass, Merrill E. and Douglass, Donna N., *Manage Your Time, Your Work, Yourself*, 1993.
- Gleeson, Kerry, *The High-Tech Personal Efficiency Program*, 1998.
- Gleeson, Kerry, *The Personal Efficiency Program*, 1994.
- Mayer, Jeffrey J., *Time Management for Dummies*, 1995.

settinG GoALs

- Hill, Napoleon, *Think and Grow Rich*, 1937, Copyright Renewed 1988.
- Murphy, Shane, Ph.D., *The Achievement Zone*, 1996.

ProbLeM soLVinG

- Bendaly, Leslie, *Strength in Numbers*, 1990.
- Bittel, Lester, R. and John W. Newstrom, *What Every Supervisor Should Know*, 1990.
- Feltman, John, *Secrets of Successful Executives*, 1991.

- Ivancevich, John, M. and Michael T. Matteson, *Organizational Behavior and Management*, 1987.

LeADershiP

- Bellman, Geoffrey, M., *Getting Things Done When You Are Not In Charge*, 1992.
- Bothwell, Lin, *The Art of Leadership*, 1983.
- Caroselli, Marlene, *Leadership Skills for Managers*, 2000.
- Josefowitch, Natasha, Ph.D., *You're the Boss*, 1989.
- Kouzes, James, M. and Barry Z. Posner, *The Leadership Challenge*, 1987.
- Manz, Charles, C. and Henry P. Sims, *Super Leadership*, 1989.
- Portnoy, Robert, A., Leadership: *Four Competencies for Success*, 1999.
- Senge, Peter, M., *The Fifth Discipline*, 1990.

coMMunicAtion

- Boothman, Nicholas, *How to Make People Like You*, 2000.
- Hamilton, Cheryl, with Cordell Parker, *Communicating for Results, 5th Edition*, 1997.
- Murphy, Kevin J., *Effective Listening*, 1992.

DeLeGAtion

- Carr-Ruffino, Norma, *The Promotable Woman – Becoming a Successful Manager, Wadsworth Inc.*, 1985.
- Heller, Robert, *How to Delegate*, DK Publishing Inc., 2000.
- Maddox, Robert B., *Delegating for Results – An Action Plan for Success*, 1990.

GenerAL interest

- Fuller, George, *The First Time Supervisor's Survival Guide*, 1995.
- Loen, Ramond, O., *Super Supervision*, 1994.

teAM buiLDinG

- Barner, Robert, W., *Team Troubleshooter*, Davies-Black Publishing, 2001.
- Bendaly, Leslie, *Strength in Numbers*, McGraw-Hill, 1997.
- Blanchard, Ken, and Sheldon Bowles. *High Five! The Magic of Working Together*, William Morrow, 2000.
- Book, Howard, and Stephen Stein. *The EQ Edge*. Wiley, 2006.
- Byham, William C., Richard S. Wellins, and Jeanne M. Wilson. *Empowered Teams*. Jossey-Bass, 2003.

- Cava, Roberta, *Difficult People*. Key Porter Books, 1992.
- Fisher, Kimball, *Leading Self-Directed Work Teams*, McGraw-Hill, 1999.
- Harrington-MacKin, Deborah, *The Team Building Tool Kit*, AMACOM, 1994.
- Huszczo, Gregory, *Tools for Team Excellence*, Davies-Black Publishing, 1996.
- Parker, Glenn M., *Team Players and Teamwork*. Jossey-Bass, 1996.
- Tjosvold, Dean, *Teamwork for Customers*, Jossey-Bass, 1993.

Chapter 20

Websites to Visit

"However beautiful the strategy, you should occasionally look at the results."

Sir Winston Churchill (1874–1965)
British politician

The purpose of this chapter is to direct you to some websites where you can get more information on various aspects of entrepreneurship.

The benefit of visiting these websites are you would get a lot of affordable information which you can apply to your ventures. These websites are also 24/7 so you have access to learning all time especially when you are highly geared and cannot sleep, you can do something useful by looking at these websites.

By learning how to use these websites you will be able to get any information at any time for almost everything.

By using the web search like google or yahoo or internet database you can get market research and product information which you would not have been able to get twenty years ago. You would have had to pay large amounts to acquire these in the past.

However it must be emphasized that as these information are free you will need to decide if those information are what you require and if it is accurate.

Sl. No.	List of Websites	Information
1	http://www.bplans.com	For business plans
2	http://www.entrepreneur.com/businessplan/	For business plans
3	http://www.indiaco.com/	For business plans
4	http://www.ecell.in/template.php?a=eureka	Entrepreneurship Cell at IIT-Mumbai
5	http://www.ciieindia.org/	Center for Innovation, Incubation and Entrepreneurship at IIM-Ahmedabad
6	http://www.iimcal.ac.in/centers/CEI/	Entrepreneurship Cell at IIM-Calcutta

7	http://www.sebi.gov.in/investor/venturecap.html	A list of venture capitalists in India
8	http://www.nenonline.org	A list of incubators in India
9	http://www.quickmba.com/entre/	About entrepreneurship
10	http://www.entrepreneurship.org/	Fostering entrepreneurship
11	http://www.zeromillion.com/	Entrepreneur's Resources
12	http://www.entre-ed.org/	Entrepreneurship education
13	http://www.wsicorporate.com/	Business Franchises
14	http://www.ediindia.org/	Entrepreneurship Development Institute of India
15	http://niesbud.nic.in/	National Institute for Entrepreneurship and Small Business Development
16	http://www.idisc.net/en/index.html	iDISC is a unique platform for Global Network Members to showcase their incubation activities and best practices
17	http://www.eonetwork.org/pages/default.aspx	Entrepreneur's Organization
18	http://www.tenonline.org/	The Entrepreneur Network
19	http://www.inc.com/	Small Business and Small Business Information for the Entrepreneur
20	http://emerging-entrepreneurs.com/	Emerging Entrepreneurs
21	http://www.powerhomebiz.com/	Information, tools and resources for starting, managing and growing a home business.
22	http://www.bioscience.heacademy.ac.uk/resources/entrepreneurship/skills.aspx	UK centre for bioscience
23	http://nysscpa.org/prof_library/guide.htm	Accounting Terminology Guide
24	http://www.accountingweb.com	Accounting
25	http://www.adweek.com	Adweek Online
26	http://www.aafd.org	American Association of Franchisees and Dealers
27	http://us.bbb.org	Better Business Bureau
28	http://www.bizbuysell.com	BizBuySell
29	http://www.bizwomen.com	Bizwomen
30	http://www.toolkit.com	Business Owner's Tool Kit

31	http://www.businessownersideacafe.com	Business Owners Idea Café
32	http://www.brandchannel.com	BrandChannel.com
33	http://www.brandweek.com	Brandweek
34	http://www.catalystwomen.org	Catalyst
35	http://www.chiefmarketer.com	Chief Marketer
36.	http://www.customerservicegroup.com.	Customer Service Group
37	http://www.customerservicemanager.com	Customer Service Manager
38	http://www.the-dma.org	Direct Marketing Association
39	http://www.eff.org/issues/intellectual-property	Electronic Frontier Foundation: Intellectual Property
40	http://econnect.entrepreneur.com.	Entrepreneur Connect
41	http://www.fambiz.com	Family Business
42	http://www.franchise.com	Franchise.com
43	http://www.franchiseexpo.com	Franchise Expo
44	http://www.google.com/docs	Google Docs
45	http://www.bea.gov/scb	Survey of Current Business
46	http://www.copyright.gov	U.S. Copyright Office
47	http://www.uspto.gov	U.S. Patent and Trademark Office
48	http://www.zimdesk.com	Zimdesk provides all the features and functionality you would expect from a standard desktop PC.
49	http://www.zoho.com	Zoho offers a suite of office tools
50	http://www.singaram.com	Our website

Part VI

Entrepreneurial Jugalbandi

Chapter 2: Entrepreneurial Means of Protecting the Fruits of Labour

"What is worth copying is worth protecting."

Chittu Nagarajan, 2005
Online dispute resolution professional

Now that you have found your vehicle you need to stir it without the fruits of your labors being robbed. As good entrepreneurs, we must give credit when due and therefore I must place on record that this chapter is based on Chittu Nagarajan's original material.

A good idea in itself is just an idea. It has no value at all until something is done with that idea. That idea has to be produced in a form / product in order to become valuable and in turn the product or service has to be commercialised.

It is a fact that when you are involved in entrepreneurship there is a high probability that you may develop something new. It may be an invention, software, design, literary work etc.

The name or brand that you may have developed will also be new. You must remember that all these have a VALUE attached to them. This VALUE is known as Intellectual Property or IP.

inteLLectuAL ProPerty

Intellectual Property Consists of :
- Copyright
- Patents
- Trademarks
- Industrial Design
- Integrated Circuits
- Trade Secrets or Confidential Information

We will take a look at each one of these later in this chapter.

Why inteLLectuAL ProPerty?

Intellectual Property Rights exist to encourage, promote and protect entrepreneurs. You do not have to be worried that someone else may reap the benefits of what you have sowed or the hard work you have put in.

It is vital to acquire your 'Rights' to an invention, work or name and then to enforce those 'Rights' in the market.

commercial Value

IP has commercial value or potential commercial value. If you protect it no one else can infringe upon it and use it for their own gain.

If you go through the process of inventing a product, process, or device, etc. you may come up with a great new name or slogan, write a company document spending the time to protect it, can save you a great deal of legal trouble.

Do some research yourself. This can save you a lot of money. The internet is a boon and so make use of it. If there is an infringement of rights, IP rights be enforced.

copyright

Copyright in India is governed by the Indian Copyright Act, 1957 as amended by Copyright (Amendment) Act, 1999.

Copyright means the exclusive right to do or authorise others to do certain acts in relation to literary, dramatic, musical, artistic works, cinematograph film and sound recordings. e.g. books, music, art, software, films etc. Literary work includes computer programs, tables and compilations including computer databases. In other words copyright is the right to copy or reproduce the work in which copyright subsists. You can use copyright to protect company brochures, annual reports, or other documents. The law does not permit one to appropriate to himself what has been produced by the labour, skill and capital of another. The objective is to encourage authors, composers, artists and designers to create original works by rewarding them with exclusive rights for a limited period, to exploit the work for a monetary gain, to protect the author of copyright work from unlawful reproduction or exploitation of his work by others. How do you benefit commercially? By licensing your exclusive rights for a monetary consideration.

Ingredients for Copyright

Ideas by themselves do not have copyright. Ideas must be expressed in material form for copyright to subsist. In order to secure copyright, the author must have bestowed upon the work his labour, capital and skill. It is immaterial whether the work is wise or foolish, accurate or inaccurate or whether it has any literary or artistic merit. What will be considered sufficient to merit for copyright depends upon each case.

The work should be original. Originality of "expression of thought" is required. The thought itself need not be original. Expression of that thought has to be original and should originate from the author. e.g. Dan Brown's "The Da Vinci Code". Ideas themselves are unprotectable under copyright. The work has to be written down, recorded or reduced to material form.

Ownership of Copyright

An author is the copyright owner. Where the making of a work is commissioned or where a work is carried out by an employee in the course of his employment, unless there is an agreement to the contrary, the copyright in the work shall be deemed to vest in the person who commissioned the work or the employer.

Registration of Copyright

No registration is required to acquire copyright. Copyright automatically subsists as soon as the original work comes into existence. Copyright protection is not granted where the work is grossly immoral, illegal, defamatory, seditious, contrary to public policy or calculated to deceive the public.

Term of Copyright

Generally, copyright subsists during the lifetime of the author plus 60 years after his death. In case of joint ownership until all owners' life time plus 60 years of the last one. Unpublished during lifetime will also have 60 years from publishing.

Necessary Elements for Copyright notice

There are four elements for copyright notice. These are

- The symbol ©
- Year of 1st publication
- Author's Name
- All rights reserved

For example,

> Copyright © 2009 Muthu Singaram. All Rights Reserved.

Berne Convention

Berne Convention for the Protection of Literary and Artistic Works is an international agreement governing copyright, which was first accepted in Berne, Switzerland in 1886.

Works created or protected in a member country must be given the same protection in all other member countries just as that country grants its own nationals. India is a member of this convention.

Other treaties in this area are UCC Geneva (Universal Copyright Convention, Geneva Act), UCC Paris (Universal Copyright Convention, Paris Act), TRIPS (Agreement on Trade-Related Aspects of Intellectual Property Rights). Membership in TRIPS coincides with membership in the World Trade Organization and WCT WIPO Copyright Treaty, Geneva. India is member a of all these treaties besides WCT at the time of writing this book.

Infringement of copyrights

In the U.S. Supreme Court case of MGM V. Grokster, it was ruled that one who distributes a device with the object of promoting its use to infringe copyright is liable for the resulting acts of infringement by third parties. Peer to peer services can be sued if they encourage users to share copyrighted material without permission.

In the recent, a Hong Kong citizen was jailed for three months, for sharing three Hollywood movies online, over the BitTorrent network. He happened to be he first person to be convicted for using the peer to peer services.

Patents

India is governed by The Patents (Amendment) Act 2005 and the Patents (Amendment) Rules 2005.

A patent is a monopoly or exclusive rights granted by the government to a person who has invented a new and useful article or an improvement of an existing article or a new process of making an article, for a limited period. The patent gives exclusive rights to make, use, sell the invention and to assign or transmit the patent via licensing contracts for a period of 20 years from the date of application. After the expiry of the duration of patent anybody can make use of the invention. The objective of a patent is to encourage and develop new technology and industry, to promote innovation and to stimulate creativity.

Ingredients of Patents

Patent must have novelty (new) and true invention. You cannot discover another person's invention and apply for patent. Patent must have lack of obviousness to a person of ordinary skill and knowledge in the related field. Patent must have sufficiency of description/ be applicable in the industry and which can be industrially manufactured or used and must be useful.

An idea cannot be patented. Only the article or the process of making some article by applying that idea can be patented. A device cannot be patented if it has been published anywhere in the world or if it has been used or offered for sale in this country prior to the date of the patent application. The patent does not give its owner the right to practice the invention, only the right to exclude others from doing so. Copying, reproducing or selling a patented invention without obtaining a license or permission from its inventor is strictly prohibited. Unawareness of existing patent is not a defense.

Applying for Patent

Before applying for a patent it is prudent that one does an extensive search to find out if the invention or process already exists.

Do not wait until your inventions are fully developed. Apply for a patent as soon as your idea of the nature of the invention has taken a definite shape.

The subject matter of patent protection has evolved as technology has developed and progressed. In recent years there has been much discussion and debate, and some confusion, regarding the patentability of living matter (non-naturally occurring forms which are the product of human ingenuity), software and business methods, but it is now well established that all these can be patented. Software and business methods cannot be patented in India. Software can only be protected by copyright.

The first person who files a patent application gets the patent, even if he or she is not the first person to invent the claimed subject matter. Only the U.S and the Philippines have a first to invent system so if you can show you will be the first, you will be granted the patent.

Patent Cooperation Treaty (PCT)

This treaty allows applicants to file an "International Application" at one's home country patent office under the auspices of the World Intellectual Property Organization. India is a member of this treaty.

Patent Offices are located at Mumbai, Delhi, Chennai and Kolkata. The Indian Patent office has brought out a Manual of Patent Practice and Procedure, 2005 and General Information Booklet for filing Patent application in India.

trademarks

India is governed by the Trademarks Act, 1999.

A trademark is any distinctive word/s, symbol, emblem, name, logo, slogan, letters, drawings, pictures, colours or combination of colours or trade dress that a company uses to identify the origin of a product or to distinguish it from other goods in the market. It may also be a combination of all the aforesaid elements. It is what the company wants itself to be identified with.......The Company's Identity. Scents and Smells can also be registered as trademark. Sounds can be used as trademarks as well as shapes and configurations of products.
   Coca Cola bottle.

Although in some countries and in some situations a mark may be protected without registration, it is generally necessary that for effective protection a mark be registered in a government office. If a trademark is registered, no person or enterprise other than its owner or authorized users can use it, infringement actions can be taken against them otherwise.

Trademarks rights can last indefinitely, if the trademark continues to be used. In India, the only criteria is that it has to be renewed every 10 years. However, the exception is - trademark rights can be diminished, eroded or lost if the owner does not continuously use the mark, or if the owner does not actively enforce his rights against known infringers, or if the trademark loses its significance in the market by becoming generic. Generic is a part of everyday language and hence becomes common. An owner may lose his trademark right if the mark becomes a generic name e.g. aspirin, escalator, yo-yo, cellphone etc. These were once enforceable trademarks but not any more now as they are common words in the English language. Why resort to trademark? To prevent others from using the same or confusingly similar trademark for the same or similar product. To prevent others from using confusingly similar marks, stripping off the identifying source and replacing it with different marks. Mere registration of a domain name does not confer trademark rights. You have to use your domain name to identify your goods or services to acquire trademark rights.

Trademarks that cannot be registered

The use of a mark which is likely to deceive or cause confusion, is contrary to any law for the time being in force, comprising or containing scandalous or obscene matter, comprising or containing any matter likely to hurt the religious sensibilities of any class or section of the citizens of India, which would be disentitled to protection in a court of law, which is identical with or deceptively similar to a trademark already registered in respect of the same goods or goods of the same description. A word which in the accepted name of any single chemical name or chemical compound in respect of chemical substances and marks prohibited under the Emblems and Names Act cannot be registered. Trademarks that have been registered already or trademarks that are pending before the Registry which are similar to the mark it seeks to register may be searched at the Registry situated in Kolkata, Delhi, Mumbai, Chennai and Ahmedabad.

Ingredients of Trademark

The name should suggest the use and nature of the product or service and should be easy for the customers to remember. Present a trademark in such a way that it stands out. Use bold letters, colours, capital letters, quotation mark and use the trademark consistently. Do a trademark search to determine whether the name is available for registration. It is common ground for people to put in a lot of time and money into developing a name only to find out later that somebody else has a right to it. It is very frustrating, hence conduct a thorough search first.

Trademarks should be used. If it sits idle for more than 4 yrs then it is redundant. Not only should it be used but it must be used properly. Use the appropriate notice symbols – TM, SM, ® – this shows that the marks belong to you.

Madrid Protocol

The Madrid Protocol covers trademark matters, and facilitates registration of trademarks in member countries by allowing proof of registration in the home country to be deposited in a Central Registration Bureau. At the time of writing this book India was not a member of this protocol.

industrial Design

Governed by the New Designs Act, 2000 in India. It features shape, pattern or configuration or ornament applied to an article. This must appeal to the "eye", must be new and be industrially applicable.

Registration is required and the duration of Protection is not less than 10 years. The International treaty which governs New Design is the Paris Convention of which India is a member.

integrated circuits

This is similar to industrial design and used for integrated circuits.

trade secrets or confidential information

Trade secrets are also known as Confidential Information. It is information, generally not known, which is valuable to the owner and kept in strict confidence or in secrecy. In recent times, trade secrets are deployed in keeping "Technology" secrets in this technology era.

Examples are customer lists, designs, instructional methods, manufacturing processes, formulas for producing products, recipes, invention and processes that are not patentable and technical know-how.

Trade secret protection attaches automatically when the information is kept secret by the owner. The owner has the right to prohibit others from misappropriating and using the trade secret. Duration of protection is as long as the information is valuable to the owner and is kept in secrecy. Protection will be lost if the owner fails to take reasonable steps to keep the information secret.

This covers all the avenues available to you as an entrepreneur to protect your idea.

GenerALLy

The legal regimes establishing ownership and control of intellectual property are applied on a territorial basis; that is, they are created by, and apply only to the country of origin. Accordingly, in order to protect your intellectual property in countries outside your own, you must establish such protection in each country.

You might think that this would require an examination of each country's laws to determine the existence and scope of protection in that country. Fortunately, many countries adhere to established international conventions and treaties mentioned above.

Many of these conventions and treaties are administered through the offices of the World Intellectual Property Organization in Geneva, Switzerland (www.wipo.org).

iMPortAnt boDies

WIPO – World Intellectual Property Organization.

TRIPS (Trade-Related Aspects of Intellectual Property Rights) by GATT (General Agreement on Tariff and Trade). TRIPS Agreement requires all GATT members to provide at least a baseline level of protection and enforcement for patents, trademarks and copyrights.

Chapter 22

Entrepreneurial Ethics

"The earth, the air, the land and the water are not an inheritance from our forefathers but on loan from our children. So we have to handover to them at least as it was handed over to us."

Mahatma Gandhi (1869–1948)
Indian political and spiritual leader

Ethics is doing the right thing as entrepreneurs. However, who decides what is the right thing? The simple and the best answer is you decide and go with it as long as it is acceptable by the law of land.

Another area where companies have started to look at is Corporate Social Responsibility CSR. Everybody think they know what CSR is. But unfortunately most people think that doing some charity work is CSR but continue to carry out unethical means of business i.e. burning material in open fire for benefit which damages the earth.

What is CSR and why is it so important? Businesses are corporates but, what makes up these? People are the main element of any business. These same people make up the society at large. As part of this society we can use any resource available from nature but with this comes the responsibility of protecting our earth and this is CSR.

We should use resource properly and return the benefit to the earth in the whole to the society so that they can equally enjoy the benefits. This is why corporates have to return to society as they are majors players in using the resources.

This a responsibility which corporate have and they must replace what they take for the betterment of future generations.

A few examples of CSR activities from the corporate are given below:

Tata Technologies Corporate Social Responsibility program

Tata Technologies is a part of the TATA group. They work with the world's leading automotive and aerospace organizations for engineering designs. The mission of the Tata Technologies Corporate Social Responsibility program is to make a positive impact on the communities with which the company does business through its support of select programs, outreach efforts and initiatives that improve and enhance the quality of life. Their goal is to make things better for the planet, better for people, better for business, better now and better for the future.

Some of the following programs have been undertaken by them.

The First Book programme. They donated 10,000 books to children of poor families. This program was run with the First Book.

The Environment Stewardship programme is to demonstrate the company's commitment to environmental sustainability and to the quality of work life for their employees. A 2.3-acre wooden site has been used to setup the headquarters. It is an open two-storey work space with maximum amount of natural light cycling programs, the use of sustainable materials and water conservation methods to reduce environmental impact.

The ready Engineer programme is to impart voluntary classroom base training on industrial experience to Engineering students of 3rd and 4th year.

Macomb Homeless Coalition Programme held each January to help needy individuals to find housing, employment, food, clothing, health care and emergency shelter. Tata Technologies staff gives time, technical support and computers on-site as resources throughout the event.

Road Safety in India programme. About 100 professionals, volunteer during peak periods to provide road safety information. *Asia Pacific Blood Donor Programme*. The staffs are encouraged to give blood.

Anand corporate services Limited

Anand is a leading manufacturer of automotive components and systems in India. They are suppliers virtually to every vehicle and engine manufacturer in India.

Anand has been committed to playing a role for the needs of the society. This is in view of Anand's belief that the benefits from the business must trickle down to the society at large for any economic development to be meaningful.

Anand believes that the corporate goals must be aligned with the larger societal goals. The SNS Foundation was setup for 25 years, in line with this. SNS foundation's objective is for comprehensive community development.

The Foundation carries out programmes in the fields of health, education, natural resource management and life skills training to ensure fellow human being lead a quality life.

Anand CSR's long term goal is to implement concepts like 'Zero Tolerance Zone for Child Labour', 'Zero Waste Zone'. It applies the 3*Rs Reduce, Recycle* and *Reuse* not only at Anand / SNSF locations but extends it to Anand residential areas.

Aptech Limited

Aptech Limited is an education player with a global presence. Aptech is participating in community activities in association with leading NGOs by providing computers for schools, education to the underprivileged and conducting training and awareness-camps.

Aptech students who sell their art work donated some of the proceeds to NGOs to promote education among all sections of the society in the country and in particular the underprivileged. Aptech partners with leading NGOs throughout the country and this includes the Barrackpur-based NGO, Udayan, a residential school for children of leprosy patients. Aptech strongly believes that education is the way forward and supports the underprivileged children in India in this area.

Avon cycle Limited

Avon is the largest cycle producer in India. Avon started MATAKAUSHALYA DEVI, PAHWA CHARITABLE HOSPITAL to help the poor in rural areas as there was no facility for the poor people and they had to turn to cities and towns. This was the reason for the late Mr. Sohan Lal Pahwa, AVON's Chairman and Principal Trustee to begin a hospital that has risen to serve a model healthcare facility boasting of some bold experiments. The hospital reaches out to the needy, farther afield it holds regular camps in surrounding villages to propagate scientific approach to healthcare. The hospital has taken the social responsibility concept to a new level by running a scheme titled 'Celebrated Female Child' to change the mindset of 'sons only' parents.

cisco system inc.

CISCO is the world leader in networking products. The company has a strong "triple bottom line" profits, people and presence. To promote a culture of charitable giving CISCO connects it employees to nonprofit organizations to serve their local communities. CISCO enables employees to develop and utilize their talents to give back to their communities for advancement of their careers. CISCO also gives technology to improve the lives of community and solutions for achieving environmental sustainability.

icici bank Limited

ICICI bank is the second largest bank in India. The ICICI Social Initiatives Group (SIG) is a full time and permanent team which concentrate on its development-related initiatives. SIG is to define and effectively fulfill its responsibilities as a corporate citizen. ICICI believes that education and health are basic needs for all people, especially the poor in order to participate in the larger economy. Easy access to basic financial services and effective use of appropriate technologies will give better opportunities to all to participate in the economy in an equitable and productive manner. This group has focused its attention on identifying and supporting initiatives in early education, health in particular to reduce infant mortality rates, microfinance and application of technology to improve life. The tough field visits aims at assessing the need and facilitating dialogue to form an integral part of their work.

infosys technologies Limited

Infosys is one of the largest IT firms in the world. Some of their initiatives are notebook distribution, distributing books and stationery to underprivileged children, behaviour and social skills development for children, medical camp and cleanliness drive. Educare launched a dedicated intranet portal to help employees support education of the children of their housekeeping and security staff. Staff helping the visually challenged volunteers regularly by conducting weekend reading sessions.

Volunteered staff constructed a water facility for rural schools to supply drinking water to 1,000 students of the Avanippoor Government Higher Secondary School. Every Wednesday is known as the day of change and people drop coins in drop boxes placed at the campus entrance and exit points, food courts and parking area.

Volunteered staffs provide Language and computer education to the security and housekeeping staff. More than 330 people pledged to donate their eyes in a special camp organised by the Ruby Hall Clinic and Eye Bank Association of India.

To boost the confidence of underprivileged children a program called Play And Live (PAL) using sports to teach them various skills and change their outlook is performed where they donate sports equipment including carom and chess boards, and give prizes such as watches, perfumes and chocolates.

itc Limited

ITC is one of India's most valued companies. It is also one of Asia's top 50 companies based on Business Week's report. ITC portfolio is diversified. They have a presence in cigarettes, Hotels, Paperboards & Speciality Papers, Packaging, Agri-Business, Packaged Foods & Confectionery, Information Technology, Branded Apparel, Personal Care, Stationery, Safety Matches and other FMCG products. ITC has had a strong presence in its traditional businesses of Cigarettes, Hotels, Paperboards, Packaging and Agri-Exports. ITC is quickly gaining market share even in its new businesses of Packaged Foods & Confectionery, Branded Apparel, Personal Care and Stationery. ITC has been partnering the Indian farmer for close to a century. To further enhance this partnership ITC has taken a new paradigm by leveraging information technology through its 'e-Choupal' initiative. This initiative takes a widening look at its partnership with the farmers by supporting a whole lot of value-adding activities programs to create better livelihoods by helping poor tribals make their wastelands productive, by investing in rainwater harvesting to improve irrigation to the dry lands. This program also empowers rural women by helping them to become entrepreneurs. ITC provides infrastructural help to make schools interesting for village children in this program and by doing so ITC touches the lives of millions of villagers across India.

Mahindra & Mahindra

Mahindra started in 1945 by assembling the Willys Jeep in India and is now an Indian multinational. It has over 1,00,000 people working across the globe and enjoys a leadership position in utility vehicles, tractors and information technology with a significant and growing presence in financial services, tourism, infrastructure development, trade and logistics. The Mahindra Group defines Corporate Social Responsibility as making socially responsible products, engaging in socially responsible employee relations and making a commitment to the community around it.

In 2005, at its 60th anniversary it renewed its commitment to Corporate Social Responsibility by pledging to dedicate 1% of its profit (after tax) towards Corporate Social Responsibility. An innovative program called ESOPs (Employee Social Options) has been launched to give employees an opportunity to be involved in socially responsible activities of their choice.

The group also announced to provide free cochlear implants to 60 under-privileged hearing-impaired children.

The Nanhi Kali is a project for the girl child and the Mahindra All India Talent Scholarship for both to provide educational assistance for the underprivileged.

Dalmia cement (bharat) Limited

Dalmia Cement started cement manufacturing in 1939. The Company carries out social welfare programs which provide health and other amenities. These programs are for the public and employees' families in the surrounding villages of their factories. These include operating schools for the employees' children, awarding scholarships to outstanding students, milk distribution schemes and other cultural activities, tournaments and games. At Dalmiapuram, the company runs a State Government recognized Higher Secondary School.

Another project Dalmia, along with Trichy based Hope Foundation, has undertaken is Quality Education, Health and Livelihood training programme for the villagers in and around.

DcM shriram consolidated Limited

DCM operates in a number of energy intensive businesses in the Chloro-Vinyl and agri-sectors. DCM's Shriram Krishi Vikas Kendras (SKVK's) programme's objective is to impart scientific knowledge to the farmers to improve their profitability covering crop cycle and harvesting. The program supports the farmers in their work and life by helping in meeting educational, hygiene, sanitation as well as healthcare support for animal husbandry.

In Kota the DCM has equipped Maharao Bhim Singh (MBS) Hospital, with a state of art intensive care unit and Private rooms. DCM runs health camps in adopted villages and centers to create awareness on diseases like AIDS and Cancer. DCM provides periodic Eye check-up by arranging camps and Family Planning programmes.

DCM provides scholarships to encourage meritorious and needy students in the fields of Engineering, Medicine, Agriculture and Management and runs a 'Primary Education Programme' for the girl child, which provides for support on books, school bags and uniforms.

DCM has also contributed for construction of school buildings both in cities and rural areas. It reconstructed the Primary School building at Gandhidham in Bhuj district of Gujrat which was reduced to rubble in the earthquake in January 2001.

Chapter 23
Entrepreneurial Talent Management

"Men often become what they believe themselves to be. If I believe I cannot do something, it makes me incapable of doing it. But when I believe I can, them I acquire the ability to do it even if I didn't have it in the beginning."

Mahatma Gandhi (1869–1948)
Indian political and spiritual leader

Talent management has become one of the most critical areas in business today. Talent management is a life process that must be developed and reviewed with the business requirement. Good talent management is about achieving change through people as they are the most vital resource for your business. A well developed talent management program can bring entrepreneurs a lot of intellectual capacity and returns which is more rewarding than providing the resources and environment that will enable your team to bring great results.

tALent MAnAGeMent: A LiVinG DeFinition

Talent management is the set of processes by which your business will identify, attract, develop and retain people with the critical skills to move your business forward. Defining key people needs for future success as part of a current strategy.

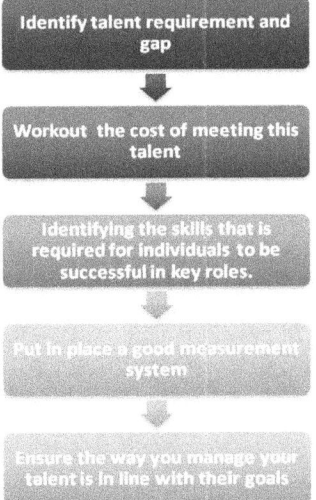

Every company is looking at the return on investment but it is very rewarding to your team to be motivated, able and achieving their full potential. The final goal in talent management is about achieving change and success through your team.

Each company approaches talent management in their own way and hence there is no set of standard practices and check lists that you can adopt. Entrepreneurs must apply a dynamic but fluid process that can change with the business for managing talent.

Why tALent MAnAGeMent toDAy

In 1990's companies started to see that talent management was important for business for many reasons. Prior to this companies looked at people as manpower planning – labour demand and supply – and it was largely a statistical measure.

Only a few places recognized talent. These include in the sports arena, movies and art studios.

With rapid changes in business and industrial structures it is important for companies to study talent. With new technology and rise of the internet, talent has become the forerunner in most companies. Most talent managers are concerned on succession plans for leadership but companies should focus on overall talent pool.

the MAJor DriVers For tALent MAnAGeMent

It is important to note that talent management is not career management for the top few but in many cases talent at work is people who run and carry out day-to-day activities.

Most companies have started to have specialist roles for management talent. As entrepreneur if you have good talent management, it can be used to your advantage. You can use it as the means of negotiating which can bring great results and change to the company.

Why have companies started to take talent management seriously is because of the following key drivers:

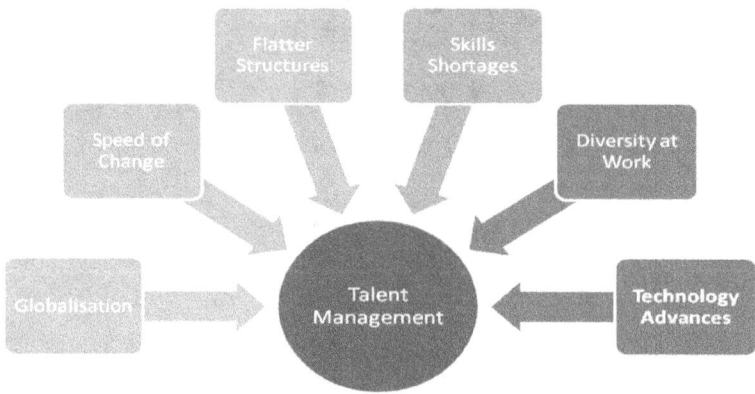

Globalisation

This is transforming companies to take a closer look at talent management. It is not only for multinational companies but it is for anyone who wants a global presence, a need to focus. Due to this, smaller companies will need to resort to specialisation to survive. It is often difficult to attract talent because they prefer larger companies where it is more attractive but with globalisation anything can happen to anyone. So this is an area where all entrepreneurs must focus on how to attract, assess and develop key talent.

speed of change

With product life cycle becoming shorter this has huge implications on talent. Because a company will need to be looking on top of the next 'big thing', look ahead at talent which can carry a company forward in the next three, five and ten years.

skills shortages

Due to the change and globalisation and several other factors we are now seeing all over the globe shortage of much needed talent. Because of this some poorer countries have benefit from migration to higher economy and outsourcing which bring much needed funds to the home country.

Flatter structures

With technology and fierce competition hierarchy is becoming more flat. And most companies are losing their talent in management and hence a huge vacuum for management persons.

Diversity at work

Due to better health care, long work life and higher number of women coming into work force there is a huge diversity in work today. Therefore it is important to manage talent otherwise people tend to move faster.

technology advances

This driver also provides methods to management talent. With increasing technology advances we need higher skills and most mundane jobs are to be done by technology. It is worthy to note what today's requirement is may not be tomorrow's requirement. So a talent management programme must take that into account.

talent Life cycle

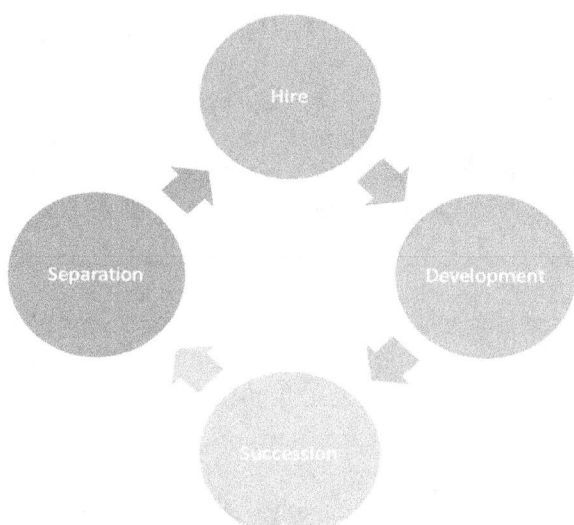

The talent life cycle once you have identified the required talent you will need to hire them. Then you need to train them. At an appropriate juncture you must plan succession and eventually separation will happen. This can be in the form of new job, company or hirer.

Chapter 24: Entrepreneurial Mentoring

"People with courage and character always seem sinister to the rest."

Hermann Hesse (1877–1962)
Swiss (German-born) author

All successful entrepreneurs have some kind of mentors. Therefore we are going to explore this area to see how we can benefit by having a mentor.

Mentor is the Latin word meaning "to endure" or "to sustain a relationship to share one's experience with others". Mentoring is a way of offering support and advice to someone and may touch on any aspect of their life.

MentorinG, coAchinG, trAininG

Mentoring is different from coaching and training. Coaching is specific and tightly focused. Training is work related. A mentor may provide coaching or training if and when required.

tyPes oF MentorinG

There are two types of mentoring. One is known as natural and the other planned. Natural mentoring comes from parents, teachers, friends and generally people we know. This form of mentoring is experienced by all of us in one form or another. Planned mentoring is when a structured program is devised where mentors are matched to mentees. This second form of mentoring is becoming more and more popular around the world.

These programs are becoming more and more popular because the people who have been mentored have given great testimonials for these programmes.

How do these programmes work? People are matched informally or formally through interviews, personal profiles, common interest, getting to know sessions etc. Mentors are usually from a varied background and are sought informally or formally.

Mentoring can be used in educational, career, personal or venture development. It can take any one of the six relationships of open, closed, private, public, formal and informal.

An open relationship is when anything is discussed; a closed relationship is when only specific things are discussed; a private relationship is one where no one else is aware expect the mentor and mentee; in a public relationship everyone knows about the relationship; a formal relationship is one where the mentor and mentee document their relationship; an informal relationship is one where there is no documentation.

Mentors have two roles one as experts and the other as role model. Mentors help mentee to learn new skills and knowledge. They help to increase the achievement rates, self esteem and confidence. Their role is to help understand social behaviours how organizations work, office politics, promote learning and explore new and conflicting ideas. They help handle setbacks and problems, gain expert knowledge, acquire new knowledge and skills, help in personal development and help in understanding changes and build value.

the MentorinG Process

The mentoring process has three simple steps.

step 1: Mentor investigates

- Builds a relationship
- Listens
- Asks open ended questions
- Plans the programme

step 2: Mentor identifies

- Challenges
- Strengths and weakness
- Priorities
- Development requirements
- Provide information and advice
- Shares experiences

step 3: Mentor Plans

- Allows creative ways of thinking
- Assist to make decisions
- Agree to plans
- Evaluates and monitors progress

PrinciPLes oF GooD MentorinG

Mentee must be willing to accept challenges, be committed to the mentoring process, be willing to learn and take risk and above all must have trust and confidence in mentor.

Mentee will gain from the challenges, friendship, learning from models, learning from errors, from listening, building self confidence and get wise advice. Beside this, mentee's get coached, get support, encouragement and become more self aware.

Mentees should not expect the mentor to manage, solve problems, tell them what to do, expect a easy ride, expect favours, gossip and end the relationship when problem is resolved.

Mentee's weakness can be strength overdone, persistentency usually will have positive results, do not treat everyone the way you want to be treated, must be different and be able to connect with others and take responsibility and willingness to take risk.

Principles of good mentoring are listen, listen and listen, understand how the mentee feels with you, start from the mentee's current position, support / tweak mentee's ideas, fill the missing links, change must be measurable and when not working, change.

Conversation during mentoring must be friendly but professional, challenging but supporting, connecting hard to soft skills, not focusing on your issues but with client's issues. Be a listener but do not just agree.

Mistakes mentors make are agreeing too early on internal conflicts, taking things personally and sharing your thoughts too early. Things a mentor must avoid, are not to tell mentee what to do to improve, not give advice outside subject expertise and not confuse mentor's issues with mentee's issues.

In conclusion, mentoring must have an incentive for the mentor, must change as time goes on and must be monitored for effectiveness

Mentoring is never one to many, it must be one to one, otherwise it is not mentoring.

Chapter 25 — Entrepreneurial Alternatives

"The weak can never forgive. Forgiveness is the attitude of the strong."

Mahatma Gandhi (1869–1948)
Indian political and spiritual leader

We have included this section to show you there are other ways to start your entrepreneurial journey and also how you will pass the baton to the next person.

You can become an entrepreneur by acquiring someone else's company. Advantage of buying a business is if it is successful it will mostly keep being successful. It would have a good location. It will have staff and suppliers. Equipment is installed and tested. Inventory and line of credit would be established. Time is saved and one can learn from the experience and it can be a bargain. Obviously disadvantage of buying a business would be the opposite. It is not profitable. It has bad will. Staff and location may not be suitable. Equipment may be out of date. It would be difficult to implement changes. Inventory may be out of date. Account receivable might be overvalued. Business might have been over priced.

stePs in buyinG A business

1. First analyse your skills, ability and interest. Then make a list of the businesses you are interested in. Then check out the list by looking for available companies. Then carry out an evaluation of the business; the reasons for selling, the state of the business, the prospects for the business, any legal issues and the financials of the business.
2. Next is to work out the value of the business. This can be done in one of these ways by looking at the Balance Sheet but sometime this could give a wrong picture. So we should look at an adjusted Balance Sheet to remove what does not appear to be attractive.
3. The other methods are by earning Approach and Market Approach.

Then negotiate to buy the business. Get it at the lowest price. Good terms of payment. Minimal upfront payment ensure the finances are accurate.. Find out what are the financing options and make sure the changeover is smooth.

DeAL structuringG

Another area often entrepreneurs miss out is how to structure a deal. Usually this is done in a hurry to get started by getting the funds but this can backfire once the business starts to boom. So a lot of caution must be exercised here especially in the areas of financial elements the stage of the business, risks at the time of existence, pricing the deal and non-financial elements and the investment agreement.

business MAnAGeMent succession

This is another area we in India do not like to speak about. Usually because it is family owned or we have fallen in love with the company.

The plan should be to plan an alternative to you, mentor them, and create an environment for a successor. Or alternatively look to sell the business internally or externally.

It has been an extremely brief chapter deliberately. Our interest here is for you to have an overview of these three areas only.

Chapter 26: Entrepreneurial Learning From Other Entrepreneurs

"Wisdom is a weapon to ward off destruction; It is an inner fortress which enemies cannot destroy."

Thirukkural 421 (200 BC)
Thiruvalluvar, the Tamil Poet

In the last chapter we talked about mentoring which can be direct or indirect. In this chapter we will talk about other successful entrepreneurs who can help you to be successful. We are deliberately using only examples of Indians, successful over the past 100 years in India, and examples of Indians who are successful overseas.

Why have we done this? To demonstrate there is no fixed pattern in terms of educational level, family background, social standing or demographics for entrepreneurship.

DhirubhAi AMbAni

India's most famous entrepreneur can be none other then Dhirubhai Ambani. He is the third born out of five to a school teacher in Gujarat in 1932. Even as a child he was out to make money. During the Mahashivratri (Shivaratri) fair, he sold Gathia (Snack) with some friends. After matriculation, at 17, he went to join his brother in Aden to work for Shell, in a petrol station, filling gas and collecting money where he was soon promoted to Sales Manager. While at Shell, he was impressed by the way the company would spend money to gather information and his dream was to build a company like that. After eight years he returned to Bombay to start a trading company with a few thousand rupees. He borrowed Rs.15,000 to start Reliance Commercial Corporation, a trading company. In those days this was a lot of money. Then he started Reliance Textile Industries and promoted the "Only Vimal" brand spending a lot of money. He ran into a resistance from the wholesale trade. So he changed his mode of supply. He bypassed them and opened his own showrooms and appointed agents from non-textile background to run these showrooms. He started franchisees. He found that there was a market untapped – the non-metro urban segment, so he started his outlet there. In 1980 a record number of 100 showrooms were opened on a single day. He came up with innovative financial models addressing the needs for small towns. He went to US to raise money because cost was lower. He hired the best and above all he never feared losing as he believed he came from nothing so he had nothing to lose. The world famous King of Bollywood, Mr Amitabh Bachchan called him as India's "first capitalist". The former

President of India, Mr. Abdul Kalam, in his lecture, *'Growth is Life'*, illustrated, using the classical Tamil poet Thiruvalluvar. That a true leader, would always defeat problems and never be defeated by them. "Dhirubhai Ambani gave problems to problems," quipped the president.

Lessons from him
- Determination
- Vision
- Be different
- Be innovative
- Look for talent
- Confidence

rAhuL KuMAr bAJAJ

Rahul Kumar Bajaj was born to a businessman in 1938. He went to Harvard for an MBA. His family was highly political. His first job was as DGM under Firodia, CEO of Bajaj Auto and MD of Bajaj Tempo. A misunderstanding led to Bajaj Auto and Bajaj Tempo splitting, with the CEO taking Bajaj Tempo and Rahul Bajaj keeping Bajaj Auto. Bajaj in 1960 tied up with Piaggio to produce Vespa. In 1971 the relation ended and they started their own with captures like "You can't beat a Bajaj" and "Hamara Bajaj". In 1972 he became chairman after his father's demise. Bajaj scooter was so popular that the black market was thriving. USA and Germany started to buy these scooters. However, Piaggio went to court on the grounds of pilfering design. Suit was settled outside court and Bajaj withdrew from the USA market. Then Honda came to compete. He appointed 100 new dealers. A good number were competitor's dealers. At this stage they had no marketing department but soon corrected it. He promoted Bajaj Auto Finance and partnered Kawasaki to compete in the motorcycle market.

Lessons from him
- Family does not mean you take over straight away
- Smart partnerships
- Know when to withdraw
- Correct your mistakes

rAtAn tAtA

Ratan Tata is rich and the first born to Naval Hormusji in 1937. Ratan is the great grandson of Tata group founder Jamsedji Tata. After his parents separated he grew up in an orphanage until adopted at 13 by Lady Navajbai Tata. His childhood was troubled because his parents would not get on and were separated. He went to Cornell and Harvard. Lady Tata taught him dignity, keeping promises and being dependable which he applied along with his work. At one instance, he refused to accept Rajan as union leader because he was a dismissed worker with a criminal record who had been dismissed for mistreating a security guard. Ratan started with TELCO and moved to TISCO before turning to NELCO and Central India Textiles.

Lessons from him
- Luck can change any time
- Values must be upheld

KirAn MAZuMDAr shAW

Kiran Mazumdar Shaw was not prevented by the male chauvinism of India's beer industry from following in her father's footsteps as a master brewer. If not for her, India would still be waiting for the emergence of its first significant biotechnology company. Kiran tried to get into the business but was faced with a lot of excuses about how its remote locations and often violent labour unions were unsuitable for women. So she utilized her knowledge of fermentation to set up what is now India's largest biotech company. But gender bias continued to dog her, she says: "Banks wouldn't lend, and even women didn't want to be my secretary. It was all about credibility—because I was a woman, not from a rich family, and with no track record". Now the bias works the other way, she says. It has helped her get a place on the Indian Prime Minister's business advisory council and on a new India-U.S. council of top company bosses. "As a successful woman," Mazumdar Shaw says, "you are in a unique position when the world is looking to be inclusive of women". Biocon's success says it all—it accounts for more than 10% of the Indian biotech industry's $1.1 billion in annual revenue.

Lessons from her
- Without being connected you can make it
- Gender bias should not stop you
- Use the discrimination to help you and not the other way round
- Use your talent

nArAyAnA Murthy

Narayana Murthy was born in 1946 in Karnataka, India. He went to the University of Mysore and IIT Kanpur. In 1981, he founded Infosys with six other software professionals. He believes people are the assets and it is the manager's job to find what drives them. The managers should share and promote others. In 1999 Infosys Technologies became the first India-registered company to be listed on an American stock exchange. He is a member of the Asia Society's International Council and Board of Councilors of the University of Southern California School of Engineering. He is also on the Wharton Business School's Asian Executive Board. On Aug 11, 2001 during the convocation address at IIT, Delhi, he said perhaps we are the only nation in the world where people fight to be called backward rather than forward.

> *Lessons from him*
> - You do not need to live outside India
> - Nor need to be educated outside India
> - People are the most important assets
> - Help and share with others

AZiM PreMJi

Azim Premji was born in 1945 and is one of the richest men in the country. He went to Stanford. In 1966 he joined Wipro, which was his father's vegetable oil business.

> *Lessons from him*
>
> These are directly from him.
> - You must have the courage to think big
> - You must not compromise on fundamental values
> - You must build tremendous self-confidence
> - You must surround yourself with the best people
> - You must have commitment to quality
> - You must play to win
> - You must be blessed by the force beyond us

K b chAnDrAseKhAr

K B Chandrasekhar is from a typical middle class, conservative joint family with parents and grand parents. His father encouraged him to learn stocks and even bought them under his recommendation at the age of 12. He started his career in Wipro, then moved to the USA via Roltas. In 1992 he started Fouress. In 1994 he started Exodous and 1999 Jamcracker. He saw the need for research and development in the areas of information sciences and life sciences, and established the Anna University – K B Chandrasekhar Research Centre (AU-KBC Research Center) in 1999 at the Madras Institute of Technology (MIT) campus of Anna University, as a collaborative venture between Anna University, Chennai (Madras), and the K B Chandrasekhar Family Foundation.

> *Lessons from him*
> - Family is important in our success
> - Give back to society

VinoD KhosLA

Vinod Khosla went to IIT Delhi and Stanford. He started Sun Microsystems in 1979 after graduating from Stanford University, and then several others. He is now a venture capitalist.

Lessons from him
• Timing is no barrier
• Starting without experience

You would have seen that these entrepreneurs come from varied background but the only thing they all have in common is to be successful entrepreneurs and that is what you have in common with them.

Chapter 27

Entrepreneurial Mindset

"The healthiest response to life is joy".

- Deepak Chopra (1946–)
Physician, Public Speaker, Author

Many of us want to be entrepreneurs not knowing really why as we only see the upside of entrepreneurship and not the downside.

We are only seeing the successful entrepreneurs and that is why we are keen on entrepreneurship but there are more people who fail than succeed. So it is not true that all entrepreneurs are successful.

You need to a have high driven motivation. Most of us would like to possess these characteristics but find it difficult to have these.

"Is this the only thing?" you may ask. To further examine these we should look at the various definitions for entrepreneurship.

There are a lot of definitions for "who an entrepreneur is". Let us look at some of those now.

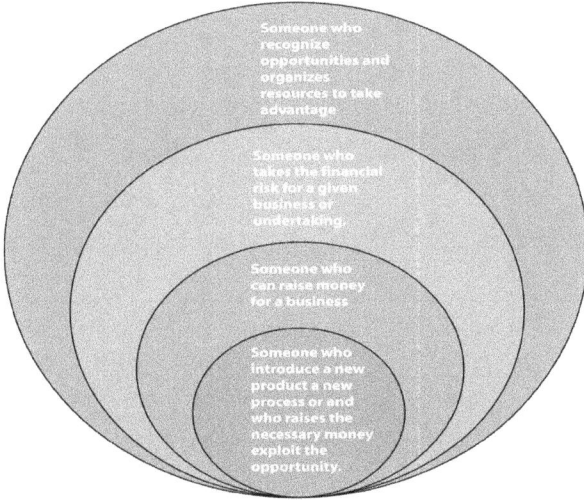

By looking at these definitions we cannot pinpoint what an entrepreneur's mindset is but what is clear is that their focus is to succeed in what they set out to do.

So, how would you know if you have the mindset of an entrepreneur? By looking at other entrepreneurs and comparing them to yourself. In an earlier chapter we have explained what it takes to be an entrepreneur. So you can try and compare yourself but please note that there is no fixed mindset.

Mindset is something certainly complex to find out and just because you are like an entrepreneur does not mean you will succeed.

Most entrepreneurs have lot of self-confidence, a sense of urgency, challenge and this drives them to success.

As we have said many times there is no set pattern but you can see that in general all entrepreneurs take risk, are self-motivated, want to achieve, are innovative, and enjoy challenges.

Sharing My Entrepreneurial Experience for the Benefit of Other Entrepreneurs

Chapter 28

"Success usually comes to those who are too busy to be looking for it."

Henry David Thoreau (1817–1862)

US Transcendentalist author

In this final chapter we are going to share with you what we have learnt in the last 15 years as entrepreneurs. This is for the benefit of young budding entrepreneurs who can be better prepared than we were when we started.

the Mbs PrinciPLe

We believe in the MBS principle, which we now apply in many of our work, and have seen considerable amount of success in applying this. The MBS is the Must, Be and Should of an entrepreneur.

Must

We will first look at the MUST part. Entrepreneurs must at least apply the following five principles in their work.

1. Have a vision and review it regularly. Unless you have a vision and review it you will not know what you are doing.
2. You must have fun and be relaxed in what you are doing otherwise success becomes difficult and a burden.
3. You need to have urgency and excitement in order to get things moving and working.
4. It is an absolute must to have time for family and prayers. When you are successful you need someone to share it with and you need to pray to have strength in times of need.
5. You need health so you must have time for exercise.

be

Next comes the BE part. Entrepreneurs should at least be able to apply the following eight principles in their work.

1. Be open. When you are open you will be able to change when things are not right.
2. You need to be willing to learn otherwise you will not gain any new knowledge.
3. You have got to be yourself and do not worry about others as no one is worried about you anyway.
4. Be able to change so you can improve and get better.
5. Entrepreneurs need to be patient to get results.
6. You must be helpful and respect others something most of us take for granted.
7. You have got to be serious and result oriented in order to be an entrepreneur.
8. Entrepreneurs need to be thankful, only then will you appreciate success.

should

Finally comes the SHOULD part. Entrepreneurs should at least apply the following six principles in their work.

1. You should know where you are heading if not, how you will succeed?
2. You should know how to handle success as most people do not become too full of themselves and become difficult people.
3. You should earn everything and not take it for granted.
4. You should not feel sorry for yourself as nobody else cares.
5. You should write positive statements.
6. Entrepreneurs should plan for the next day at the end of each day.

These are not the only principles but we found these most helpful and have been able to improve ourselves and our productivity by applying these simple yet useful principles.

We hope that this humble book made your reading worthwhile. In the event you have found it useful please let us know. Again if you think there are ways we can improve this book please let us know. And if you feel it is all Rubbish that is fine too. Let you be the judge of that as the book must be of value to you and Only You. Thank you

Muthu Singaram, the entrepreneur on his journey for making more entrepreneurs along with the contributor to this book Chittu Nagarajan.

www.ingramcontent.com/pod-product-compliance
Lightning Source LLC
Chambersburg PA
CBHW082106220526
45472CB00009B/2067